Zelia Raye.

Founder and creator of the Imperial Society of Teachers
of Dancing's Modern Theatre Faculty.

ZELIA RAYE
And the Development of
MODERN THEATRE DANCE

by
Pamela Eddleston FISTD

With an introduction
by Mary Clarke

DANCE
EXAMINATIONS
BOARD

Published by the
Imperial Society of Teachers of Dancing
2002

Published by the Imperial Society of Teachers of Dancing
Imperial House, 22/26 Paul Street, London EC2A 4QE

ISBN 0-9543220-0-2

Published in Great Britain 2002

All rights reserved
Printed and bound by Biddles Limited of Guildford, England

For Mrs A

Acknowledgements

For today's musical theatre dancers – students, teachers and performers alike – this little book charts our roots.

It could not have appeared however without the drive and dedication of Murielle Ashcroft, Chairman of the Modern Theatre Faculty from 1974 to 1998, who instigated the project. She envisaged a "small, slim volume", a biography of Zelia Raye as a record of her legacy to the dance profession in general and to the Modern Theatre Faculty in particular.

Mollie Webb initially researched, sorted and logged the available published material about Zelia from Dance, The Dancing Times, dance journals, personal letters, birth certificate and reminiscences. It was Mollie who uncovered "Zelia's" real name and background.

I was given this material four years ago and, fascinated by it, continued to develop the project and write the text. Murielle Ashcroft took the first, very rough draft to Dancing Times editor Mary Clarke and, encouraged by her, we pressed on.

Ann Hutchinson Guest, who had been a dear friend of Zelia, gave suggestions and assistance and generously submitted her reminiscences of Zelia as did Moyra Gay, along with valued comments during the subsequent drafts.

Mary Clarke kindly agreed to write the introduction, setting the innovative work of Zelia and Joan Davis in its contemporary context.

Finally, Paul McFarland offered to oversee the fulfilment of this most important dream of Mrs Ashcroft, editing the text and integrating photographs and illustrations ready for printing, and arranging publication, and Mark Wilson based his cover design on my favourite photograph of Zelia.

I am also indebted to Sir John Mills for permission to include part of his biography "Up in the Clouds - Gentlemen Please" and to the Dancing Times for permission to include old articles and photographs: very few originals remain but Elaine Mayson managed to reproduce many of those in the book from the bound volumes of Dance and Dancing Times.

Others have also read the drafts and commented, including Sheelagh Harbinson, Daphne Peterson and Sarah Wilson.

To all the above, family and friends, I extend my grateful thanks for their encouragement and support.

Pamela Eddleston
August 2002

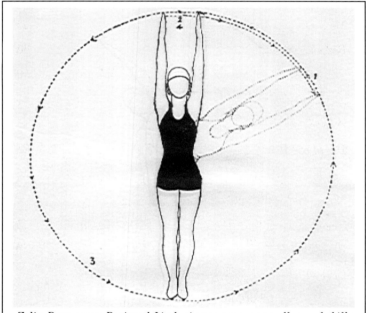

Zelia Raye wrote Rational Limbering to encourage all-round skills in dancers and teachers – "my advice to those who would make a financial success of their art". The ISTD published it in 1929

Contents

Introduction

All the contributors to this book have dealt with their personal and individual memories of Zelia Raye yet all agree on one aspect of her personality – her vision.

The dance world here in the 1920s was very different from that of today. There were innumerable studios, innumerable teachers, innumerable openings for dancers in what was then called musical comedy and in the many pantomimes which flourished, annually. throughout the land. The pantomimes employed, in addition to the troupes of professional dancers, cohorts of "babes" who tapped and sang their merry way through their first appearances on stage.

It was a busy scene, but also one that lacked cohesion. It was Zelia Raye, more than anyone I believe, who, through her work, brought these different elements together under the aegis of the Imperial Society, and recognized how important and influential could be the example of what was to grow into the Modern Theatre Faculty of today.

Looking back, and looking especially through the pages of Dancing Times which consistently, thanks to Philip Richardson's

Zelia Raye's book on American Tap Dancing was published in 1936 with striking modern illustrations by Lovell

faith, charted her work, we can recognize how steadfastly Zelia Raye shared her knowledge and enriched our understanding of what was being brought to fruition in the world of theatre dance in countries throughout the world.

I knew Zelia only towards the end of her long and active life, but I quickly realized that she was, even then, still looking forward. She was aware of what was happening in the American modern dance movement from its earliest days, and understood how the new theories of movement and dance techniques being developed there could be put to the service of theatre dance in this country.

It was this constant search for knowledge which kept her so young and made her such an enchanting and stimulating companion.

Zelia showed the way, but her lasting memorial will be not so much in the pages of this book as in the achievements of the generation who followed her and laid such a firm foundation and inspiration for the teachers who belong to the Modern Theatre Faculty of today. In saluting her, we also salute them, for it is through their devotion that the work lives – and grows – today.

Mary Clarke

The Life of Zelia

One of the most popular and successful faculties of the Imperial Society of Teachers of Dancing is the Modern Theatre Dance Faculty.

What exactly is Modern Theatre Dance? Where did it begin and how did it evolve? What was the thinking behind it?

The answer to these frequently asked questions is inextricably linked to Zelia Raye, who founded and inspired this unique dance education. The basis and foundation of her work has endured into the 21st century, appealing to the changing spirit and expression of dance styles in the theatre since the 1920s.

It continues to thrive and grow; an incredible phenomenon when one considers that a syllabus was never actually created as such, but rather it evolved while maintaining the original integrity of Zelia's methods and ideals.

This is a tribute to a dynamic and imaginative woman, far reaching in her vision, astute in her sense of business, uncompromising in her quest (and demand) for excellence, and boundless in her energy and interests.

It is also a tribute to the talented people who contributed and developed this vision with dedication and devotion.

The legacy that we now call Modern Theatre Dance is recognized worldwide.

The Early Years

1900-1927

Zelia Raye was born Bertha Reid in Blackburn on September 1st 1900 to Ellen and John Reid, a cotton weaver. Bertha Reid's early years and dance training are something of a mystery. The first connection with dance of which we can be certain is a delightful photograph of her in November 1916 in The Dancing Times, which indicates that by 16 she had left home for the bright lights, and was a pupil of Carlotta Mosetti, a well known dancing teacher in London.

In 1920 she is seen as principal dancer in "Goody Two Shoes" at the Kilburn Empire Theatre using the eye-catching name of Zelia Ray. Sometime between March and July 1921 she added the "e" to make it "Zelia Raye" - by which she was known for the rest of her life. Then followed various productions including several with the Italian Opera Company, "Louise," "Thais," "The Barber of Seville" and "Faust."

Zelia would have received a thorough and technical dance training under the tutelage of Carlotta Mosetti, a "male danseuse" who had partnered many famous stars of the ballet including Adeline Genee and Phyllis Bedells. From 1904-1909 Miss Mosetti had been ballet mistress of the Alhambra Theatre, famed in the West-End for its lavish opera and ballet productions.

In this rich and eclectic theatre environment, Zelia developed her passion for dance in all its forms. It was a time of great change in all aspects of life. In the theatre world, old time music hall was being taken over by the more refined, sophisticated forms of entertainment such as Variety and Revue. It was a time when stars of the ballet might find themselves on the same Variety bill as singers, acrobats, speciality acts, even animal acts. It was the time of Diaghilev, the great impresarios, Moss Empires, Stoll circuits.

Variety was big business. In 1920 a Moss tour comprised 24 theatres; a Stoll tour 17 halls; and so, armed with good looks, determination and a strong technique, Zelia secured a variety of engagements; and she flourished.

In 1920 Zelia was dancing at the Winter Gardens Blackpool. The Dancing Times reported: "Some capital solo dancing by Zelia Raye, whose technical ability is of high order..."

She was invited to pose for photographs to illustrate Dr. V A P Coghill's article "Anatomy For Dancers" published by The Dancing Times. These photographs show clearly her strong, supple physique and confident stance.

She travelled to St Moritz to appear in cabaret and to arrange various dancing entertainments. Seemingly, Zelia was one of the few English dancers to appear in variety shows in Italy at that time and, to add to her repertoire, she included Italian folk dances. She was constantly searching for new ideas to develop her craft and to give her a performing "edge." This was to be the pattern of her life.

While in Italy she formed a partnership with another English dancer, Quentin Tod, and together they arranged a series of exhibition dances, which they took to Spain.

In July of 1921 Zelia was principal dancer in "Gypsy Princess" at the Prince of Wales Theatre in London; Quentin Tod again appeared with her in a speciality duo. By this time Zelia Raye was becoming well-known and successful in the profession. She was arranging many of the ensembles for musical shows, dancing the solo roles and acting as ballet mistress. She was responsible for the productions of the second and third editions of the "Nine O'Clock Revue," starring Beatrice Lilly and Anita Elson, and "Head over Heels" and "Island King" at the Adelphi Theatre.

As she moved more into the field of producing and directing, she became increasingly aware of the need for well-trained dancers for her shows. In January 1927 she began teaching

MISS ZELIA RAYE

On the back of this postcard Zelia wrote: "Life is change and don't I know it! This card will amuse you" and gave it possibly to Joan Durrant.

musical comedy classes in association with the Arts Studio. Six of her students secured professional engagements, Olga Morini and Nita Glynne at the Plaza; Miss Linstead and Miss Archer in "Time Flies," Kathleen Mitchell in "The Last Waltz," and Miss Vaile in "Sunny."

Her classes proved so popular that she transferred to 77 Oxford Street, W1, and extended them to three afternoons a week.

First Visit To America

1927-1930

In 1927 Zelia took the first of her many trips to the United States, which were to prove so influential to the thinking and development of her craft, and which consequently had a profound effect on professional dance and the teaching of dancing in England.

She visited New York, Washington, Chicago and Los Angeles, writing excitedly of her experiences and the wonderful work that she saw. She met many well-known celebrities and visited prestigious schools such as The Denishawn School, The Ernest Belcher School, Nicholas Tsukalas and Dorothy Mackill at the First National Studios.

She was tremendously impressed with the all-round training that American dancers received, particularly the technique of stretching and limbering, and the use of syncopation. She was excited by the floor technique, which at that time was extremely innovative. She greatly admired the emphasis that Americans placed on personality, style and individuality in performance.

Wasting no time on her return to England, Zelia put a large advertisement in The Dancing Times, introducing her American Methods and wrote a long detailed article (see pp. 67-70) extolling the virtues of American training and showmanship.

This first trip was to become the catalyst. Zelia, with sharp business acumen, set about marketing these new ideas with fresh vigour. She embraced wholeheartedly the teaching practices she had discovered in the USA and adopted an American accent. Indeed, many people believed her to be an American. Zelia had anticipated, and stimulated, a trend.

1928 saw both her production work and the studio blossom. Early in the year she produced "Blue Skies" for Charles Heslop. Amongst pupils booked for shows were Eileen Fowler (later of TV fame), as principal boy in pantomime in Exeter; Rosamund

Belmore, on tour with "Punch Bowl," Nita Glynne and Amy Gillespie, on tour with "Show Boat" and Eileen Archer in "The Irish Follies."

By March the studio had moved to 12, Little Newport Street and Errol Addison was engaged to direct the operatic dancing – the term for what we now know as classical ballet - in the school. The engagement was an astute move. Errol Addison was a well-known classical dancer having performed with the Diaghilev Ballet. He was also principal of the Cecchetti School of Dancing and performed regularly with his partner Gertrude Mitrenga, who also assisted him with the teaching. Thus the classical ballet side of the school was assured and strong.

While Zelia was now collecting a formidable staff of teachers, it must be noted that they all continued to work as professional dancers; Addison and Mitrenga performed at the Palladium and also in "Running Wild" at the Carleton Theatre, while Zelia kept busy producing dancers for the opera season at Covent Garden, the new "Mistinguett" show at the Moulin Rouge and numerous other cabarets and musical comedy.

The increase in staff made it possible for her to offer special daytime classes for professionals and dance teachers. Operatic classes were held in the mornings and musical comedy, stretching and limbering in the afternoons. The school thrived, and classes were well attended - especially the popular afternoon classes of limbering and stretching, a "must" for the professional dancer.

By June 1928 Carl Barnard was added to the staff to assist in a managerial capacity. He was a young West-End actor, at that time appearing in the "Grand Guinol" at the Little Theatre. Zelia was now able to build up an agency alongside the school, which proved very successful in providing cast members for the imminent production of "The Tavern Maid" and for productions with the big theatre companies.

Zelia arranged additional numbers for the show "Queen High" for Bannister Howard and following this, she offered rehearsal classes, specialising in her modern American methods and toe-buck dancing, to dancers appearing in the West End. Toe-buck numbers had become popular in musical comedy shows and consisted of tap dancing on the tips of the shoes, rather like musical pointe work, very uncomfortable and treacherous to the knees but nevertheless fashionable, and a necessary skill for the musical comedy dancer.

A charming article appeared in the Dancing Times in December of that year written by Zelia and entitled, "Modern Spectacular Dancing" (reproduced pages 70-73). Although dated by the standards of today, it gives a true insight into a musical comedy dancer's world in the 1920s.

Certainly, she kept an eye on the practical and commercial perspective but she always stressed and thought deeply about the inner feeling of the art.

In this article she gave tips on: "Giving Auditions: Have Lovely Legs: Make Dancing Pay": "...Now do not let us lose sight of the fact that it is possible for a dancer to have marvellous technique and very little else...............Without feeling, dance is meaningless."

1929 proved to be a bumper year for the development of the studio and production. Additional evening classes were given by Ailne Phillips while Errol Addison continued to give morning classes even though he was performing at the Kit Kat Club, Cafe de Paris, in "Lucky Girl" and in the Lyceum Pantomime. This sounds impossible, but typically the stars at that time sped from theatre to theatre in taxis, changing en route.

Zelia was so engrossed in the growth of the school and agency that she actually turned down Alan Foster's offer to go to the United States to do some producing for him. But the success of her enterprise was attracting many artists who later became famous in the theatre. One of these, booked for "Nunky's Club," was the young John Mills. Mills' career began in musical theatre: his elder sister was a close friend of Zelia's, and in his autobiography he pays Zelia due tribute for the key role she played as he sought his first break. (reproduced pages 55-58).

It was around this time that the talented, incomparable Joan Davis appeared on the scene to assist Zelia. In addition to fulfilling her own London engagements, Joan Davis was a most important and influential force in the success of Zelia's projects during the next few years and, subsequently, in the development of the Stage Dance Branch of the Imperial Society. She was talented, she was a beauty and she was already an accomplished artist in her own right. Joan became the perfect instrument and image to present the discoveries which they made together in the productive years that followed.

In July 1929 they produced a full 45-minute programme at the Palace Theatre on Election Night. In the cast were Iris Rowe and Michael Arnand, Errol Addison, Rosamund Belmore, Aimee Gillespie (who later danced with Frederick Ashton at the Trocadero), and Joan Davis, who also compered.

It was a time when Zelia Raye

Errol Addison

14

was much in demand; she had indeed anticipated the market and was setting the trend.

The Imperial Society of Dance Teachers, as it was then known, had been founded some 25 years earlier but the 1920s saw it expand and develop with separate branches being established in key dance disciplines - Operatic (i.e. ballet), Ballroom, Cecchetti, Greek, Natural Movement. It was natural for the Imperial to start looking at musical theatre and just as natural that the Society invited Zelia to demonstrate her methods on limbering, stretching and musical comedy work, at the annual Summer School, and subsequently offered to edit a book she was writing on limbering and stretching; a development of an earlier article in the Dancing Times (reproduced pages 67-70). The demonstration was most successful with nearly 300 members in attendance.

In October 1929 her book, "Rational Limbering" was published by Cecil W. Beaumont, on behalf of the Imperial Society of Teachers of Dancing.

The Dancing Times February 1930 wrote: "...It consists of a clearly written description of nearly forty different exercises, graded in order of difficulty, and all doubt as to how these exercises should be performed is removed by the very clear line drawings by Eileen Mayo, which illustrate the principal movement of each exercise. Limbering in the hands of an inexperienced teacher might be dangerous. A careful perusal of this book, which should be in the hands of every teacher, will show how much can be safely done by a pupil in the way of this very active exercise without causing injury by damaging the muscle fibres, ligaments or joints. In some ways it is the most useful of all the recent publications of the Imperial Society."

Thus was the beginning of a wonderful, unique form of dance that has been nurtured and continually developed by many brilliant teachers throughout the decades, to become the present Modern Theatre Dance of the ISTD.

At home and abroad

1930-33

The studio was thriving. Toe-buck and Rhythm Dancing was so popular that extra classes had to be added in the evenings.

Zelia and Joan took well-earned holidays in Switzerland. They loved winter sports, particularly skating, and so early in 1930 skating lessons were also offered through the studio, instructed by Miss Gladys Hogg.

In January of 1930 Zelia and Joan Davis went to Paris to seek out new material and, always thinking ahead, they returned with original ideas and costume designs to offer artists for whom they were producing new numbers. The year passed in a flurry of activities and engagements. In July, some of their pupils had secured engagements with the Jack Hulbert and Sophie Tucker Show; others were seen in a series of "Sound Film Shorts."

In September Zelia was again teaching at the ISTD Congress. Dance Journal in September 1930 reported: "Among other things she initiated those present into the art of writing dance routines quickly, and this should prove a boon to those teachers who wish to make notes of numbers and steps and have only a very limited time to do so..."

The ability to write down or notate dance was not generally practised by dance teachers in the 1930s and so, once again, Zelia proved to be ahead of her time.

The report continued: "...Also judging by the great improvement in the Limbering and Stretching done at the Congress, Miss Raye's book on this work must be a great help to followers of this branch. The Imperial Society will shortly be forming a section for this type of dancing".

On October 31st 1930 Zelia and Joan left for a tour of South Africa, where Zelia was to produce "Moonshine," an 'intimate revue' for Charles Heslop and Joan was to play leading lady.

They also hoped to give classes there. The studio in London was left in the capable hands of Ursula Preston, who had been trained by Zelia, and had assisted her for some time.

While Zelia was with the show in Johannesburg, the Home Page of "The Star," ran excerpts from Rational Limbering entitled, "Stretch Limber and Keep Your Figure:"

"...Although her method has been accepted as a foundation technique for dancing, in her studio in London Miss Raye has made a special feature of classes for society and business people which are very popular as a form of health giving exercises, and Miss Raye is providing a short but comprehensive series of exercises for readers of The Star which will appear on this page weekly.

"...Miss Raye... is recognised by the Imperial Society, London, as the authority on the more advanced forms of physical and beauty culture which are now proving so popular."

She was also featured large in The Cape Argus on Wednesday February 11, 1931:

Zelia Raye Gives Dancers some Good Advice
Engagements that are awaiting
Ballet Performers in Cape Town

"... Miss Zelia Raye, the professional dancer, spent this afternoon at the Opera House giving Cape Town girls an audition. A ballet troupe is wanted for permanent engagement in the city theatres..." This article also goes on to give an account of Zelia's theories on the merits of limbering as explained in "Rational Limbering."

Following this successful tour of South Africa and armed with drums and a new understanding of rhythms, together with their films on African War Dances, the adventurous pair travelled extensively through North America gathering more material. They returned to England in October 1931 filled with ideas and motivation from the two continents.

17

18

Again Zelia was ahead of the market. This time she brought back "Rumba" and "Snaky Hips" and immediately set about presenting these new moves in classes and workshops.

They also brought with them the precursor of the video camera for taking moving pictures so that they could have a permanent record of their routines.

They wrote a long and detailed account of their New York visit in the Dancing Times edition of December 1931 in which they talk of dance conferences, the spacious and attractive studios, studio theatres, dancers being in high demand and with excellent pay and of the Billy Pierce Studios and Buddy Bradley.........."Rhythm with the feet; strumming on the ukulele or a few blue chords on the piano; you can't leave an atmosphere like this without getting that *something* which makes tap dancing so much nearer the artistic than one can imagine possible."

They wrote at length about Ruth St Denis, the original pioneer of modern dance in America, and her three-day concert to 20,000 people under the stars at the Lewisohn Stadium. "The Prophetess" in which Miss Denis appeared in the title role was an "allegorical dance drama; a symbolical study in mass movement of the opposing forces of humanity." (reproduced pages 77-81).

However, the biggest American influence on Zelia Raye was Doris Humphrey whose technique and philosophy were to have a long-lasting effect on her teaching and on the vocabulary and quality of movement of her future dance syllabus. Force-suspension-relaxation, breath control, dynamics, the ebb and flow of movement, inner rhythm: these were integral to the technique of Doris Humphrey. It was all very new, still part of the experimental *modern* dance movement and worlds away from British musical comedy. This manifestation of feeling and quality into movement was to have a profound effect upon Zelia. One of her favourite sayings was "feeling makes the form."

Ever practical, upon her return to England, Zelia moved her school to larger premises and set up a dance centre for professionals at 77 Dean Street W1. A large advertisement was placed in The Dancing Times. "The Dance Centre" boasted two floors; the first contained a large, airy dance studio for classes and could be rented out for rehearsals; the second floor comprised a lounge, writing and tea room, and dressing rooms equipped with shower and, to be way ahead of her contemporaries: "Modern percussion and vibrator machines are available to restore tired muscles and weary limbs and those who join the "Centre" may attend the limbering and stretching classes for a merely nominal additional payment."

The Dancing Times in March 1932 recorded that: "Miss Raye and Miss Davis returned from the States not very long ago with all the very latest developments in Step, Tap and such like work "potted" in their own moving picture apparatus ready to be shown to their pupils."

Previously, it had published an article (pages 82-84) in which they enthused about this emerging technology. One cannot help but wonder what a wonderful time they would have had today!

The new premises on Dean Street were opened by well-known musical comedy star, Jack Hulbert, who referred to the brilliant and up-to-date work taught by Zelia and Joan Davis and described himself as one of their keenest, most admiring and slowest pupils. He praised their gift of being able to analyse steps in such a way that a learner could easily understand. Many of the dance routines featured in his film, "Jack's the Boy" with his wife Cecily Courtneidge, were arranged by Zelia and Joan.

The Hulberts were household names of that time, revered in the theatre and loved by audiences for their entertainment. The Imperial was fortunate to have Jack Hulbert as Honorary Vice-President of the Stage Branch in 1933.

Zelia and Joan's arrangements of "Snaky Hips" and "Rumba" were used in another successful film for Gainsborough pictures. Also, a new act was arranged for two of their own pupils, Dorothy May and Lola Kaye, with Mary Skeaping, a pupil of Margaret

Craske. They were called "Les Trois Originals" and had a very successful opening at the Grosvenor House Cabaret, later transferring to Daly's Theatre.

Mary Skeaping appeared again amongst the notices of engagements secured for dancers, this time as principal dancer in John Hart's pantomime at the Princes Theatre Bristol. Janet Cram appeared in "Crazy Month" at the Palladium.

These young dancers were to become very well known in their respective areas of the dance world having had a sound apprenticeship with Zelia in many aspects of the theatre. Classes were held at the studio in the evenings and special courses arranged for teachers and their assistants from the provinces.

Meanwhile Zelia was at the heart of the new Stage Branch of the Imperial Society which was finally established in 1931; the first committee was formed in 1932 and the first examinations were held in 1933.

Zelia lectured at the Imperial's Congress in the summer of 1932 giving a concise account of the work of the newly formed Stage Branch and an example of a tap routine, published in "Technical Schools" of Dance Journal August 1932.

In October the Dancing Times reported the introduction of 'counter-rhythm' in tap dancing: "...A very interesting development in stage dancing, particularly in up-to-date musical comedy, cabaret and revue. Like the majority of innovations connected with this style, this hails from the States. Miss Zelia Raye and Miss Joan Davis were good enough to explain to me what it consists of:

"A bar of music consists of a certain number of beats, and in ordinary tap, whether for two or an ensemble, the performers as a rule 'come in' on the same beats. When 'counter rhythm' is introduced the dancers 'come in' on different beats, or, if they commence together in, for instance, a bar of eight beats, one section may have a 'pause' for the last two beats. Of course when they are working together they are doing similar steps. This gives

considerable light and shade to the sound of the beats, and will be found most effective when used by two or four dancers...

"Miss Raye always believes that fours are the best numbers for intricate work, and when there is an ensemble of eight or sixteen, the actual steps and movements should be simple so that they can be done in absolutely perfect rhythm. The mere lifting of one knee three or four inches too high will spoil the general effect."

This 'counter rhythm' technique was immediately used in the dance routines for "Southern Murmurs" at the Court Theatre Liverpool and other musical shows. It was all the rage at that time and was quickly incorporated into the new Stage Branch. In December 1933 an article appeared in Dance Journal entitled:

Elementary Tap Rhythm By Zelia Raye

"The Tap Technique, as used by the Stage Branch of the ISTD, has been compiled to simplify the teaching of this type of dancing which, apart from its popularity, is proving a very successful method of teaching rhythm.

The terms have not been devised to baffle the mind of the student, but will be expressive words, which themselves almost explain what is required in the step. They are the material from which there is an unlimited field for designing steps and routines-the count being the pattern weaver.

There are many steps in Tap Dancing, which are dangerously alike. Dangerous, because this form of dancing can be made into a hopeless, rhythmless jumble, and yet these same steps, if properly executed, are the keys to the musical expression. As Mr. Jack Hulbert says: "It is quite interesting to take an old step and twist it round to an original rhythm..."

Zelia was intrigued by rhythms, their complexities and possibilities. It is no wonder that the Modern syllabus has a unique approach to the subject and a section devoted to its study and development.

Spreading the work

1933-39

Although Zelia and Joan had been teaching their "new" methods of stage dancing for several years it was not until July 1932 that the work was officially incorporated and issued in a syllabus. It is notable that in those early years, it was principally for the assistance of professional artists, teachers and senior students with no hint of the wonderful children's work, which was yet to come.

Originally the Stage Branch was established for the purpose of:

- bringing its members in touch with the theatrical profession;

- developing and maintaining a high standard of modern stage dancing; and

- assisting qualified members in obtaining professional engagements.

A General Meeting of the Imperial Society of Teachers of Dancing was held at Knightsbridge Hotel, London on January 8th 1933. The President, Major Cecil H. Taylor mentioned that the first examinations of the newly formed Stage Branch were to be held on January 21st and 23rd. He advised the meeting that the Council had that morning been pleased to nominate Miss Zelia Raye and Miss Joan Davis, Mr. Freddie Lord, Miss Italia Conti and Miss Mollie Suffield as Fellows of the Stage Branch Committee, with Mr. Jack Hulbert as the Vice-President.

So officially began the journey towards the Modern Theatre Dance that we know today.

The February issue of Dance Journal reported that those contemplating entering the Stage Branch... "may be interested to know that there are three grades of examinations and two kinds of certificate, according to whether the successful candidate takes the examination as a teacher or as an artiste.

The following table will make the scheme clear:

Examination	Teacher	Artiste
Grade A	Licentiate	Advanced Certificate
Grade B	Member	Intermediate Certificate
Grade C	Associate	Elementary Certificate

The quality of work seen at the first examination held for entrance into this Branch proved very satisfactory. The next examination will take place at Head Quarters on July 29th and 30th 1933."

Among those examined that year were - Associates: Mary Archbutt, Janet Cram and Winifred Lack. Member: Nina Bodenham.

In this original format, the major syllabi comprised four sections of which Musical Comedy was compulsory. The optional subjects were Tap, Modern Ballet and Acrobatic, and candidates could choose to be examined also in any or all of these.

Full stage make-up was required, and appropriate dress: something fairly tight for the limbering, with a long, diaphanous skirt and heeled shoes to be put on for the dance movements.

In April 1933 Dance Journal reported;

"After the hard work that has been put into the organising of this new Branch it is gratifying to all concerned that, even in this early phase, it should be creating so much interest. Overseas teachers from South Africa and Australia now visiting this country are working hard at the Syllabus, as they feel it is what is required to raise the standard of work and to satisfy the dancing outlook of their respective countries.

The ambitions of the Branch are very high and full of the desire really to raise the standard of Stage Dancing, so that through the Society it will be recognised and supported by the

Theatrical Profession. To this end the enthusiasm and search for new work must be kept up all the time.

Those interested in a class on the first Sunday of every month for this purpose should write to the Secretary of the Branch (Miss Joan Davis, 77 Dean Street, London W1), so that if enough applications are made, the organising of these classes can be put in hand at once."

The Studio continued to thrive both in supplying dancers and arrangements for professional theatre and in the training of

Zelia Raye : Head over Heels at the Adelphi Theatre, 1923

25

dancers for the stage using the methods now included in the newly formed Stage Branch. Zelia arranged the dance numbers for Anna May Wong in the film "Tiger Bay".

Janet Cram and Winifred Lack became assistants at the School, which was now the spiritual home and practical training ground for all those who wished to qualify in the Stage Branch.

The work was spreading far and wide including South Africa, Australia, and India, where it was reported that Marjorie Leigh, having gained her "B" Certificate, would teach and fulfil some theatrical engagements. Nina Bodenham left London in March to open a school of dancing in Johannesburg and later became known as the "mother of tap dancing" in South Africa.

Back at the studios, a room was equipped with Hanovian Alpine Sun and Sollux Lamps:..."These are a Tonic Radiation, with Quartz Light and Luminous Heat Ray Apparatus, for the promotion of muscular tone and maintaining general bodily fitness."

This 'Health-from-Sunlight' department was supervised by Mrs. Alexander and proved a very popular part of the school's work, especially during the cold weather!

Joan Davis became increasingly involved in producing and appearing in cabaret. She had her own troupe at the Tricity Restaurant and became ballet mistress of the shows at Drury Lane. In addition that year a new troupe of eight girls was formed known as "The Zelia Raye Girls."

Zelia was elevated to the position of Vice-President of the Stage Branch while Mary Skeaping accepted the vacancy on the Committee. Zelia and Joan were invited to hold a series of syllabus classes at Headquarters at six shillings (i.e. 30p) per two-hour class (numbers to be limited) and they continued to lecture for the Technical Schools of the ISTD.

Zelia continued to analyse dance, particularly in the field of aesthetics and rhythm, and to write for Dance Journal.

The First Children's Syllabus

In 1934 the seeds were sown for a children's section of the Branch. Winifred Lack was given the task of organizing the children's classes and it was made a speciality of Congress that year with exciting demonstrations given by the Bedford College, the Cone School, the Grandison Clark School, the Moreen Lawrence School and the Robinson School. The concept was met with great enthusiasm and interest especially from overseas teachers with large numbers of young pupils.

There was, in that year, an extremely valuable exchange with the Congress of American Dance Teachers. Walter Keenan, who ran a large studio in Philadelphia and was also on the faculty of the Lucille Stoddart School in New York, passed the Stage Branch Examination. He expressed great interest in the tap technique of the Syllabus and hoped to further it into an international method. The London visit of the group of American teachers, headed by Lucille Stoddart, coincided with Stage Branch Day of the ISTD Technical Schools and the visitors were treated to a warm and entertaining welcome. The American teachers were delighted with the demonstrations of the children's work.

With typical enthusiasm, Zelia embraced everything that was current in the dance world for her syllabus; now, it was the theories of Dalcrose, which can be seen in the strong rhythmic element plus those of Rudolf Laban, seen clearly in the employment of space, pattern and direction and in the emphasis on movement qualities.

In December 1934 the requirements of the children's examination were published, although these appeared to be exceptionally vague for 'analysis', and indeed left a great deal for the teachers to interpret. But her basic theories were sound and subsequent development of them into a creative syllabus was shaped by the ingenuity of talented individuals yet to emerge on the scene. Each generation embellished and extended Zelia's foundation and theories to give clarity to the technique and an appropriate look and style to ever changing demands of theatre and fashion.

Meanwhile the Raye-Davis productions were still going strong, in fact dancers for their shows and agency were in such demand that a special course was introduced at the studio to teach "Rhythm, Personality and Showmanship," in the hope that 'suitable' girls could be trained and employed.

Janet Cram was engaged to assist Joan as ballet mistress of "Glamorous Nights" at Drury Lane, and later she was given the responsibility of producing and arranging the dances for the tour of the show.

Errol Addison was elected to the Stage Branch Committee while Joan Davis became increasingly involved in theatre production.

It was reported in January 1936 that 100 girls were booked for production. Anne Stevens, now on permanent staff, was taking the classes during Zelia and Janet's absence and in July, Betty Oliphant, who later became the Founder of The National Ballet School of Canada, also joined the staff to specialise in coaching for Stage and Cecchetti examinations. Freddy Carpenter, a close friend of Zelia, taught at the school and also produced the dances for Cicely Courtneidge's film "Everybody Dance." The school supplied the dancers.

At the same time, Zelia was working on a tap technique book "American Tap Dancing" which was published by the Dancing Times in July 1936.

Sadly, by August 1936, the indomitable team of Zelia Raye and Joan Davis had come to an end. Joan was in great demand both in the theatre and as a teacher. She opened her own school in Great Newport Street and continued to develop a huge following and great respect in the theatre world. Despite the split with Zelia she maintained her close involvement with the Stage Branch, steering it through its early years and continuing to lecture and write articles for the Society. Joan Davis is still remembered with love and devotion. Hers is yet another story. In September of that year the Stage Branch membership boasted 6 Fellows, 10 Licentiates, 21 Members, 37 Associates; a grand total of 74. There were a large number of entries for the New Syllabus applicable from July 1st. The future of the Branch seemed assured. Two years later membership had jumped to 446. Dance Journal reported there had been 352 Professional Examinations and 340 Grades. Zelia was very pleased with the result of her first "Teachers Week" and there was a big demand for *American Tap Dancing*, especially from South Africa.

Tom Parry joined the teaching staff in addition to partnering Janet Cram in cabaret. There was also an influx of ice-skaters at the studio as Zelia had devised a special series of exercises especially for skaters. She loved her winter-sports holidays and it was following a Swiss holiday in January 1937 that Zelia, with Janet Cram, stopped over in Paris to see the show she had directed at the Chatelet. Producing the show was Shelagh Elliott-Clarke, the well-known and very popular dance and drama teacher from Liverpool who was later to become influential in the development of the Branch and subsequently its Chairman.

Zelia continued to arrange the dances for many cabaret acts and pupils were booked for her show "And So We Go On."

During the 1930s the schedule was very busy for all of her staff. They were expected to continue to develop the Stage Branch Syllabus, coach teachers for examinations, in addition to arranging, producing, directing and, in most cases, performing in professional engagements. In fact the high standard of dancing in theatre as a whole was being attributed to the influence of ISTD Stage Branch training.

Zelia's tireless search for influences and global connections attracted worldwide interest. In November Margaret Einert, recently returned from a study of the subject in the USA, gave a lecture on "Modern Dance" in the Raye Studio. In February 1939 Miss Rachel Buck visited from Buenos Aires to collect new material following her success in teaching the Stage Branch there. The work certainly had international appeal from its beginnings and again, Zelia prepared for another world tour that would take her via San Francisco to Australia where she planned to organise an ISTD Stage Branch.

In California she spent precious and valuable time at Mills College, renowned for its nurture of new modern dance ideas and legendary modern choreographers. Here in 1939 she filmed informal footage of these dance legends. One piece shows Jose Limon, Charles Weidman and Doris Humphrey, who walks by the camera followed by three students doing movement exercises while Katherine Manning plays tom-toms. This rare footage, "Bennington School of the Dance at Mills College," is now housed in the Dance Collection of the New York Public Library for the Performing Arts.

Meanwhile, in London, her school continued to flourish under the careful teaching of Janet Cram and Tom Parry who gave special teachers' classes, lectured at Congress and published papers for the Technical Schools.

AMERICAN TAP DANCING

BY
ZELIA RAYE

VICE PRESIDENT STAGE BRANCH I.S.T.D.

SKETCHES
BY LOVELL

Published by Order of The Council
The Imperial Society of Teachers of Dancing Incorporated
70 Gloucester Place, W.1

The War Years

During the early days of musical theatre there was great enthusiasm in the dance world. Everyone seemed to know each other. Those who endured were adventurous, there was a new world to explore, theories and techniques to be tested, boundaries to be pushed. The studio at 77 Dean Street was a well known gathering place, bustling with personalities, teachers, students, artists, the famous and the aspiring. It was alive with chatter, auditions, rehearsals, classes, and overseas visitors.

Then came the war and the world changed. Performing artists donned uniform; many were called up to join the armed forces; many more entertained the troops with ENSA (Entertainments National Service Association), or Stars in Battledress. Among them was Freddie Carpenter, by now much respected as a choreographer of West End shows. He joined the Royal Air Force, but continued to direct a number of shows and films featuring West End stars.

Zelia Raye spent the war years in Australia where she had travelled in 1939 by way of the USA. The studio in Dean Street was left in the care of Janet Cram and Tom Parry but in January 1941 this had to close "due to the circumstances," London was being heavily bombed, and a new studio opened in Staines with Olga Webb.

True to her enterprising spirit, Zelia was busy teaching and gathering new material during her Australian years. She made many friends there and cultivated great interest in the Stage Branch. She became involved in the Children's Library Movement in New South Wales and lectured to New Educational Fellowship on "The Importance of Being Rhythmic." Ultimately her enthusiasm and drive culminated in an affiliation with the Federal Association of Australia and New Zealand.

Meanwhile, on the home front, the development of the Stage Branch during the war years was in the hands of teachers who were to become its pioneers ; Marjorie Davies, Janet Cram, Tom

Parry, Shelagh Elliott-Clarke, Victor Leopold and Doreen Austin. They lectured on behalf of the Stage Branch and created routines for presentation at Congress or for publication in Dance Journal. Their strong and individual personalities carried the work and its potential still further. Also on Committee at that time were Joan Durrant, Olive Ripman and Mollie Suffield.

Zelia returned to London in 1945 and was present at the Council meeting on November 4th when the future policy of the Stage Branch was set out.

In 1946 the Committee consisted of Molly Suffield, Victor Leopold, Shelagh Elliott-Clarke, Olive Ripman, Marjorie Davies, Joan Durrant, Janet Cram, Doreen Austin and Murielle Ashcroft,.

Examiners were Mary Skeaping, Tom Parry, Joy Bury, Mary Archbutt, Joan Watts, Betty Oliphant and Nancy Robinson. It was to these dedicated individuals that the future of the Branch was entrusted after the war years.

In 1947 Zelia submitted her resignation from Council and later in the year, as the result of incorporation, her title changed to Honorary Vice Chairman and Founder of the Stage Branch. The Branch grew ever stronger. Entries for the Society's examinations in 1948 were reported "so great that the Stage Branch, 517 candidates, has had to be arranged over a series of weekends."

Another illustration for Rational Limbering –there were 38 in total, drawn by Eileen Mayo

Modern Dance in the 1950s

The 1950s saw the work of these modern dance pioneers come to fruition as dance in the theatre reflected their great choreographic influence. Zelia, always having been an admirer and advocate of this early modern movement, welcomed eminent and innovative dancers to lecture for the Stage Branch. Each lecturer infused fresh ideas, challenged and inspired members, pushed the boundaries of thinking and helped to shape and broaden the work of the Branch

Sigurd Leeder, one of the leading figures of the modern dance movement in Germany, gave a tremendously successful class at February Refresher in 1951.

Dance Journal reported: "The Stage Branch were also in force, under the Chairmanship of the indefatigable Zelia Raye, to welcome Sigurd Leeder - and once again this Branch produced a great success. One of the biggest classes which I have ever seen in the "Imperial" rose to be instructed when Mr. Leeder took the floor, and how he worked! And how the class worked! And what enthusiasm when he finished! His dance notation was a revelation - and the hope was freely expressed that Mr. Leeder will be available for Congress."

In March a reception was given to honour Hanya Holm, a leading pioneer of Modern Dance in America, well known in musical theatre for her choreography of "Kiss Me Kate." She was accompanied by Ann Hutchinson, her assistant dance producer, and Director of the Dance Notation Bureau of New York. Also present were Hope Ryrie, the President of the Federal Association of Australia and New Zealand, and Mary Skeaping who was ballet mistress of the Sadler's Wells Ballet at The Royal Opera House, Covent Garden, from 1948 to 1952 and then for nine years director of the Royal Swedish Ballet..

Ann Hutchinson Guest was to become a life long friend of Zelia Raye (see reminiscences pages 48-52).

Also in 1951, Zelia suggested and encouraged the formation and development of the first Stage Branch Group. This was to be another milestone in the development of the Branch.

Dance Journal 48 reported ..."Thanks to her far-seeing policy, (the Stage Branch Group) has been the means whereby teachers have met and conferred together, thus proving the value of co-operation as a means of maintaining and improving the standard of this Branch."

Original members included Miss Joyce Percy, who was to become a much-loved Chairman of the Imperial Society of Teachers of Dancing; Daphne Peterson, who with Joyce Percy became Director of the Bush Davies Schools; Sheelagh Harbinson, Committee Member for over 30 years; Patricia Hutchinson, Principal of the London School of Contemporary Dance; Doreen Bird, Founder of the Doreen Bird College; and Moyra Gay (the Group's first secretary) who would later be a driving force in the development and analysis of the Tap Dance section of the Branch.

This Group was the beginning of what we have come to regard as the essential regional network of groups that gather regularly all over the country for workshops and teacher support, to learn and to review syllabus.

In March 1952 Zelia created a new Modern Ballet syllabus, designed for the professional student, in order to keep abreast of the demand in the professional theatre for modern dance/modern ballet techniques.

"...This syllabus has been compiled taking into account that the candidate has already passed a major examination in ballet technique. The plus values she stressed were limbering and the discipline of time rhythms as applied to the skilled technique of ballet. She also stressed the importance of understanding the rhythmic principle applied to all subjects of the Stage Branch.

Those taking part in the two large classes showed an appreciative understanding of the work given."

In September 1952 the incorporation of modern ballet into the syllabus was given further strength by a lecture at Congress by Mary Skeaping who, despite a hectic rehearsal schedule with the Sadler's Wells Ballet agreed to give one of her delightful lectures on "The Modern Ballet."

Mary Skeaping featured a great deal in the early days of the Stage Branch. She danced in Zelia's early productions and became one of the first examiners of the fledgling Branch. She went on to become the Director of the Royal Swedish Ballet. Every year at Congress the Stage Branch had devoted its first day

Miss Zelia Raye, who has now returned home after a long stay in Australia, seen here with Chieftainess Waikianga Tipene

to technical lectures, while the following day had been kept for more diverse subjects.

During the 1950s these days became very exciting. Lectures and classes were given by the most current personalities in theatre, film and television, their various styles and up-to-date ideas were absorbed into the fabric of the work. Among lecturers in this decade were Elsa Brunelleschi, Richardina Jackson, (the Katherine Dunham Company), Paul Draper, Gillian Lynne, Dougie Squires, Margaret Maxwell, Jack Billings, Sheila O'Neill, the TV Toppers, Rudolf Laban, Lisa Ullman, Louis Conrad, Ruth Posner, Valentine Zeglovski, Ivor Meggido and many others.

In 1956 a further Modern Dance Syllabus was created by Louis Conrad to challenge the more advanced candidates

These were vital years. Dance in film and the theatre had entered a new phase and had acquired status. Dance was no longer a pleasant 'divertissement.' It had become an essential element in musical theatre, as important to the show as the music and the story. "Oklahoma" on Broadway was the turning point followed by "West Side Story" and later "A Chorus Line" and a host of other dancing musicals. Dancers had become more sophisticated and accomplished in many techniques. Ballet and modern dance, previously regarded as opposing techniques, were blending into a unique form of theatre dance. It was essential for students to have the best training in all dance techniques and the Stage Branch was at the forefront of that training. Original members of the Stage Branch Group and Committee had established schools, which were by this time developing into prestigious vocational schools with excellent full time training, and the Modern Stage Branch syllabus was integral to that training.

Zelia Raye's original foundation, her philosophy and ideals, continued to be practised, but they were being kept fresh and current by the breadth of training and the variety of teaching in those schools.

Resignation

In 1957 Zelia Raye resigned her position as Chairman of the Modern Stage Branch because she wished to be released from the administrative burden this entailed. She remained as "Founder and Past Chairman"...

Dance Journal 72 reported: "It would be natural to assume, following her resignation as Chairman of the Stage Branch Committee of the Imperial Society, that Zelia Raye was relinquishing some of her interest. After all, for many years she has been a leading spirit of the Branch, keeping fully in touch with all the rapid developments and ramifications in stage dancing, and acting as an inspiration to many young teachers.

"When I spoke to her last month however, Miss Raye told me that far from taking less interest, she was as keen as ever. In fact, she seemed to me to be really cock-a-hoop at the prospect of now being able to serve on the Committee and to express strong opinions, no longer muzzled by the neutrality of Chairmanship.

The Branch is now to be served under the joint Chairmanship of Mrs. Olive Ripman and Miss Marjorie Davies."

Marjorie Davies, a Fellow of the Imperial's Stage and Ballet branches, and a Member of the Cecchetti and Greek branches, was also a Director of the Bush Davies School famous for producing students of quality, style and outstanding excellence, many of whom went on to achieve success in their own right. A vital and brilliant lecturer and teacher, she was much loved by her students and the work she pioneered still goes from strength to strength as shown in the Star Tap Awards today.

Olive Ripman, a truly remarkable personality, was co-founder with Grace Cone of the Arts Educational Schools. She was at home in every aspect of the dance world and was a great and innovative teacher. She was also the originator of Ballroom Formation Dancing. She had great strength of character (only ceasing to ride at age 88 because her horse died!). She was admired, respected and loved by students and colleagues throughout the world.

Marjorie Davies and Olive Ripman held this position from 1957-1970.

Zelia was honoured with the Imperial Award at the refresher course on Sunday 9th March 1957. This was an award created by Council in 1956 to recognise outstanding services to the Society.

"The Council when granting the Award, wished to acknowledge the many years of selfless work which Miss Raye had devoted to the Branch she had created whereby it had become the second strongest Branch of the Society." (Dance Journal 75)

The Branch continued to grow and flourish with ever more popular lecturers at Congress to include Daphne Peterson, Joyce Mackie, Janet Cram, Tom Parry, Gwen Carter, Ruth Posner, Sesha Palihakkara, Dougie Squires, Tony Mordente from West Side Story, Malcolm Crane, Ivor Meggido, Eileen Fowler, (a former student of Zelia during the 1920s and now of television Keep Fit fame.)

Zelia continued her close association with the Stage Branch and remained technical and artistic adviser.

Another of Lowell's illustrations for American Tap Dancing

The 1960s

This decade was to see the emergence of a new generation of personalities and creators in the Modern Stage Dance Branch, a revised layout and procedure of the Professional Syllabus, a new Children's Syllabus which became a unique and popular training method in many more countries, further development of established modern dance techniques within the syllabus, and in 1965 the inaugural Janet Cram Award.

This would be the decade of Mary Archbutt, who together with a small committee and in close liaison with Murielle Ashcroft and her pianist Katherine Barlow, compiled a syllabus, which gained acclaim throughout the world for over 30 years, by providing artistic, in-depth, and appealing modern dance training for children.

Moyra Gay gave further analysis and challenge to the tap technique while Joan Hardy and Joyce Mackie presented additional contemporary material following their studies in New York.

The original members of the Stage Branch Group, Daphne Peterson, Doreen Bird, Patricia Hutchinson, Moyra Gay, were emerging as powerful lecturers and gifted teachers. The Branch which Zelia had developed was now 30 years old, maturing and cleverly evolving with the times.

In 1969 the word "Stage" was dropped from the title of the Branch as it was felt that it no longer accurately described the work of the Branch, especially in the syllabus for children. In this was recognised the growing influence of modern or contemporary dance which had changed the syllabus and the expression of the work.

Important changes to the children's examinations were also made this same year. Separate tap grade examinations were developed; until this time tap had been an optional subject within the basic grade examinations of the Stage Branch.

The Junior Tap Tests were revised; optional routines, which had been in use since 1958 were replaced by set amalgamations.

Anita Foster and Victor Leopold resigned from the Committee, Patricia Crail and Sheelagh Harbinson were co-opted to fill the vacancies.

Congress continued to draw exciting lectures and classes from eminent theatre personalities including Gillian Lynne, Hans Zullig (from the Joos-Leeder Company), Ethel Winter (Martha Graham Company), Ben Stevenson, (Houston Ballet), Peter Baker and the Bluebell Girls as well as from the talented teachers of the Branch. Among these was a young teacher, Betty Laine, whose vocational school Laine Theatre Arts is now synonymous with the training of brilliant young dancers and musical theatre artists.

Zelia retired to live in Torremolinos with her sister Zetta but continued to take great interest in the Modern Dance Branch. Despite a hip operation she remained well and agile.

Sadly this was the time when the Stage Branch lost its original luminaries, Janet Cram and Marjorie Davies, but the memory of the wonderful work they helped to develop lives on in the annual awards which bear their names. The Janet Cram Award and the Marjorie Davies Star Tap Award have become highlights in the calendar of the Modern Theatre Dance Faculty and have served to showcase the excellence of training and theatre craft of the Faculty for thirty years.

On the death of Marjorie Davies Zelia wrote;

"She was one of the first teachers to be interested in the Stage Branch and I was always aware of her loyal support and co-operation. She had a gift for creating interesting work. As an examiner and lecturer and, since 1957, co-Chairman of the Stage Branch, she contributed much to the development of the Branch. How she will be missed."

Moyra Gay wrote on the death of Janet Cram: "Very occasionally there will be someone whose passing leaves a gap that is almost impossible to bridge, and Janet Cram was just such a person. To pay tribute to her is not easy, for she was never one to want nor accept compliments, preferring indeed "actions to words" and getting on with the job while others would still be discussing and arguing, all too often getting nowhere at all.

"Janet Cram will be long remembered for her honest, unwavering approach to everything she did. There is no one who has over the years given me more encouragement and belief in myself - no one whom I would rather emulate."

In 1970 Shelagh Elliott-Clarke became Chairman but sadly only for four short years;

Upon her death in 1974, Zelia wrote: "She was one of the first teachers to support the Modern Stage Branch of the ISTD when it was formed in 1931. She was an enthusiastic and capable organizer; she gave unselfishly of her services as chairman of the Branch and will be greatly missed. I write this with a very sad heart."

Olive Ripman wrote;

"The dance profession as a whole and the ISTD in particular are bereft of a great artist and an outstanding personality. She was known all over the world as a brilliant teacher, and for creative ability and imaginative productions. Her great insight into the theatre, and her dynamic approach to everything she did made her school in Liverpool one of the most important in the country covering all aspects of theatre work.... she did tremendous work for the ISTD Modern Dance Branch"

The Last Thirty Years

A new era began. In 1974 Murielle Ashcroft became Chairman of the Modern Theatre Dance Branch and under her astute and visionary leadership the work of the Branch flourished throughout the world to become the most popular Branch of the ISTD.

The ideals of Zelia remained the bedrock of the work, but the rapidly developing demands of the big musicals had to be met and a broader creative faculty was needed to expand horizons still further. A huge period of development then followed.

The first invitation was to Daphne Peterson whose inspiring and artistic approach to the work of the Branch throughout many years made her the ideal person to create a new Advanced Modern syllabus. This used the first pre-recorded set music commissioned from Clive Chapman (keyboards) and Don Lawson (percussion).

Gwen Carter and Moyra Gay created the new Senior Tap Medals giving an extended range for the tap dancer. Brilliant demonstrations of this new work excited the audience at Congress and received standing ovations.

In order to challenge and showcase the most advanced Gold Star Medal tappers, in 1977 Murielle Ashcroft and her committee ran the first annual Star Tap Award, dedicated to the memory of Marjorie Davies. It was felt to be a fitting tribute to one who had given a unique approach to dance, technically sound yet with an appreciation of presentation and performance.

Marianne Jepson devised six different levels of Popular Tap Tests, especially for adults and teenagers. This was a whole new venture and proved so popular that some years later Medal Tests were added to the series and its success was clearly shown in the summer of 1994 when over three hundred adult tappers took to the floor at the Festival Hall Tap Extravaganza.

Sheila Tozer was responsible for introducing specialised work for boys, which culminated in the Boys Theatre Associate Examination. Alison Willett developed the work further and incorporated it into the present syllabus.

The Tap section was revised; Heather Rees, Pat Ellis, and Gwen Carter created a new approach to the technique. This coincided with a theatrical tap revival and now accounts for one third of the Faculty's activities.

As the popularity of both the tap and boys' work increased, sub-committees were formed from creative members of the Modern Theatre Dance Faculty to provide additional material. Well-known professional dancers/choreographers and theatre stars were invited to arrange sequences in unique and current theatre styles: among them Carol Ball for the Tap syllabus and Petra Siniawski for the Modern.

Daphne Peterson was joined by Doreen Bird, one of the earlier members of Council and keen advocate of the Modern work, to update the Intermediate Modern syllabus, and later, the Elementary Modern syllabus in collaboration with Christina Ballard and Sarah Wilson. Martin Koch, West End musical director, composed and recorded the set music.

In 1983 a development team was formed to tackle the demands of the aerobic craze, and Body Focus was born, complete with logo, sweatshirts and much media hype and huge success. This was reflected in its serialisation in the Sunday Express. Zelia would immediately have recognised the parallels with the popularisation of her own Rational Limbering almost half a century earlier. This talented young team - Christina Ballard, Barbara Evans, Lyn Richardson, Francesca Waite and Sarah Wilson - continued to influence the Branch's work and a new Pre-Elementary Modern syllabus, with commissioned score by Martin Koch, gave an excellent framework for the relaxed style currently in demand. Following this, The Team, joined by Tereza Theodoulou, produced an introduction to Jazz, through Bronze, Silver and Gold Jazz Awards.

The Janet Cram and Marjorie Davies Awards reached new heights in this period. The Janet Cram Award was Zelia's brainchild and originally run by the committee. However, it was Joan Durrant, examiner, committee member and Zelia's close friend who became inextricably linked with both events. She devoted her time and organizational skills to giving them a brilliance and quality that are their hallmark today. Both Awards now showcase the very best that can be seen in the work of Modern Theatre Dance Faculty.

Most recently, from 1996 to 1999 the Team, together with Katie Morea, Justine Murray, Alison Willet, Karen King and Ian Waller, now affectionately called "The Dream Team", combined to produce a brilliant and creative revival of the Modern grades. This completed a whole update of the work: in 25 years a whole new generation of teachers had produced over 40 new syllabi for both girls and boys: an incredible achievement.

Throughout the 25 years of her chairmanship, Murielle Ashcroft nurtured and cherished the legacy entrusted to her by Zelia Raye. She recognised the needs of the present day and identified people with the energy and ability to fulfil them. Modern Theatre Dance became one of the most vital and celebrated dance faculties of the Imperial Society.

At the end of 1998, Murielle Ashcroft retired, and the Modern Theatre Dance Faculty was entrusted to the care of Patricia Crail, already Chairman of the International Committee. Miss Crail had herself devoted more than 25 years to pioneering and developing the work internationally and was instrumental in extending and enriching its worldwide appeal.

Zelia Dies

Sadly Zelia did not live to see her brilliant ideas and vision develop into the new millennium. She died in 1981...

Murielle Ashcroft wrote: "With the death of Zelia Raye in June, the Modern Theatre Dance Branch lost its founder and creator, a warm, generous and unique personality. Despite absences abroad, her influence was immense and it seems unbelievable that that dynamic little figure with the American overtones and persistent demand that we refute the "shoddy" and work only for what we believe in, will not encourage us any more.

She had an exploring and acquisitive mind, was an avid reader and interested in all forms of art. Her ability to see Modern Theatre Dance as "Quality of Movement" (when others looked upon it as musical comedy) made her a legend. Her creed was that every movement should have meaning and purpose. She always insisted that the expressive feeling of dance was indispensably connected with rhythm and her unique analysis and development of this subject not only forms one of the most important aspects in the Modern work, but also inspired a technical and rhythmical approach to Tap.

The same foundation was a strong factor in helping to create a syllabus that could be developed from beginners to advanced.

She had a fertile mind and quite extraordinary intuition, but never quite came to terms with the patience and understanding required to be a great teacher, so that one had to catch the pearls of wisdom that literally fell like rain at any moment of the day (frequently as she drove through the traffic lights at red!) and apply them to a more technical basis, in order to harness the brilliance that was Zelia.

In 1958 when she retired to live in Spain, she never lost interest in the many developments of the work and her faith and encouragement constantly inspired the small but brilliant group who have striven so faithfully to propagate her work."

and the very steep section could have been lethal, even had I had snow tyres. The nearest neighbour kindly drove us to Lee to catch the train to New York. Zelia made the whole thing an adventure; she always knew how to travel light and she wore a pair of socks on her hands to carry her suitcase on the long walk back to civilization.

Being way ahead of her time, Zelia embarked on taking films on her travels. I was so impressed with her collection, particularly the shots she took at Mills College in California in 1939, footage of such modern dance greats as Martha Graham, Doris Humphrey, and Jose Limon, that on my return to New York I wrote an article for the *Dance Observer* about the need for dance films. Not too long after, the organization Dance Films. Inc. came into being and established an archive of all available films for people to rent.

Zelia was a catalyst, bringing people together, making people aware of what else was going on, making links, befriending dance visitors from abroad and introducing them to the London scene.

Zelia related strongly with La Meri, an American dancer and researcher with great style, who had made a special study of what were then called "ethnic" dances, establishing the Foundation for Ethnic Dance. Both believed strongly in 'inner technique'.

From her scrap book Zelia would send me excerpts from time to time, all interesting, all illuminating. "Let your life dance lightly on the edges of Time," a quote from the poet Tagore.

When she and her sister Zetta retired to Torremolinos they wanted to simplify things. They had a single bedroom flat, a spare bedroom for visitors would have complicated life. But they were most hospitable in other ways. They also pared down on belongings. Zelia would advocate "Belongings are a burden, be free of them!" She was the first person I ever heard say "Isn't it a good thing that we grow old! We play a different role and give room for the younger people to flourish!"

51

What a positive, uplifting person! How much I regretted that when I married Ivor Guest and came to live in London that was just the time that she retired to live in Spain.

Zelia - dancing at the Arts Studio

Moyra Gay

ZELIA RAYE Founder and creator of the Modern Theatre Dance Branch ... How often one has read those words, yet how rarely has one paused to consider their implication. Sadly a whole generation has now grown up without knowledge or appreciation of this lovable, unique and dynamic individual, who not only created the Modern Branch but also, by her untiring enthusiasm and refusal to accept anything less than the best, set a standard which has made the Branch one of the strongest in the Society.

It was in 1928 that an article written by Miss Raye was published in the Dancing Times. "Limbering and Stretching" was the forerunner of that immensely popular book *Rational Limbering* published in 1929 to be followed in 1936 by the equally successful *American Tap Dancing*. By this time the Imperial Society had realised that here was the right person to form a Stage Branch and in 1932 the idea became a reality. Now, seventy years on, one may be able to assess the immense value of all that has been achieved.

Miss Raye remained as Chairman of the Branch for 26 years, and during that time lectured, taught and examined all over the country. In 1950 it was her suggestion that "groups" should be formed in order that teachers could meet together, pool their ideas and have lessons not only from the examiners (and in those early years so much valuable help was given freely by Miss Raye and her examining board) but also by guest lecturers who would open new avenues of thought to the young teacher. Herein lay the key to Miss Raye's success for she was a performer first and foremost, and realised how small becomes the world of the teacher unless she is continually stimulated by new ideas. Her own theatre experience as a dancer and later as a choreographer gave her a wealth of knowledge, which she willingly passed on to those who worked with her. Perhaps her favourite pupil was Janet Cram, who was not only able to appreciate and benefit from the sheer genius of Zelia's mind, but was able to harness it to a unique understanding of the analysis of her work, so that there was perfect fusion between the technical approach of the teacher, and the thinking, feeling dancer. Today this is exemplified in the standard and breadth of the work presented in the Janet Cram Awards.

It is difficult to see beyond the genius which undoubtedly Zelia was, to that other person, the warm hearted immensely generous *human* being, but perhaps this can best be summed up by someone who through his work in the theatre, and by his integrity in that work has won the admiration, love and respect of so many people.

Sir John Mills not only knew Miss Raye, but in his early days was trained by her as a dancer. In his autobiography he describes his experiences with her and pays heart-warming tribute.

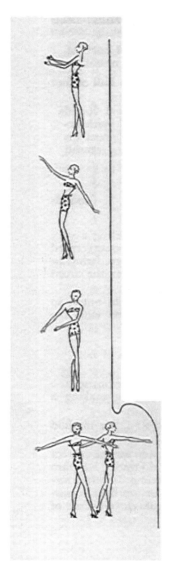

Pattern and technique – sketches from Zelia Raye's American Tap Dancing

Sir John Mills

(extracts from Up in the Clouds, Gentlemen Please)

Annie [his sister] left me another letter addressed to a Miss Zelia Raye, a great friend of hers who owned the Zelia Raye School of Dancing, which was opposite the stage door of the London Hippodrome. Zelia Raye was vital, exciting and a wonderful teacher. She had been a great friend of Annie's for years, and asked me what she could do to help. I explained that I was at the moment suffering as a commercial traveller to keep a roof over my head until I could get a job on the stage. I explained that I could dance a little but that I needed to learn tap-dancing which was a must before one could get a job in the chorus. I suggested that if she would take me on and give me three or four lessons a week, I would repay her by giving her five per cent of my salary when I started in the theatre, for the next ten years. Zelia looked at me, and her eyes twinkled. She said, "You know, if you're lucky, that could amount to an awful lot of money. Do you think it's wise?"

I said, "Well, of course I do. I haven't got the cash to pay you, and if you're willing to take a gamble, I'd consider it most generous of you."

"Right," said Zelia, "it's a deal. But we don't need a written contract. Annie's my greatest friend, so let's just shake hands on it."

....

By this time I had become proficient enough at tap-dancing to attend auditions in an endeavour to get a job in the chorus of a musical comedy. I soon discovered what a rough racket it was that I was trying so hard to join. I always seemed to be either, from the producer's point of view, too young or too short, or too tall, but never right.

Just when I began to feel I should never make it, another lucky coin dropped in my plate: during one of the evening classes

Zelia told me that she'd heard through the grape-vine that there was to be an audition at the London Hippodrome for a new musical in about a month's time. One of Zelia's other pupils, whom I had never met, was a girl called Frances Day, and Zelia suggested that it might be a good idea if she worked out a routine that Frances and I could do together. She thought it might catch the eye of the producer who would be expecting the usual solo routine.

....

She (Frances Day) was devastatingly attractive, and I discovered later on, when I was in a show with her, that the men in the audience simply couldn't take their eyes off her. She also had a terrific character; for instance, when Zelia suggested that Frances and I should work on a routine for this audition for places in the chorus, Frances immediately said that she had no intention of taking a job in the chorus; she intended to audition for the part of leading lady. She further indicated that in no way would she give an audition on the stage of an empty theatre, and to our amazement, she said that she intended to ring up R. H. Gillespie, who at that time owned the London Hippodrome, and say that she wished to give the audition with her new dancing partner at any variety theatre under Mr. Gillespie's control in front of an audience with full orchestra.

I could see that Zelia, who was used to being startled by members of the profession, was quite flabbergasted by this audacity. You can imagine, therefore, with what astonishment we heard that Frances had succeeded. She informed us that she had arranged with Mr. Gillespie that we should appear in the bill at the New Cross Empire and do our act there in a week's time.

....

We worked like slaves on the routine and finally Zelia and Joan Davis, her assistant. declared themselves satisfied.

[after the audition they were both offered places in the chorus of "The Five O'Clock Girl"]

56

I had tried to imagine for years what life in the theatre would be like, and never in my wildest dreams was it as exciting and wonderful as it turned out to be. It seemed to have everything I wanted, and nothing that I disliked. I was not shut up like a caged animal in an office for fifty weeks out of the year, and I was not trudging the streets trying to flog toilet paper that nobody seemed the slightest bit interested in.

Zelia, of course, was thrilled and so was my mother. My father, however, was still very sceptical, although I could see that he was surprised that I managed to land a job so quickly. After a discussion with Zelia it was decided that I should try and persuade an agent called Vincent Earne to handle my contract for the London Hippodrome. Zelia said that although I had landed this job on my own it was vitally important for a young actor to be in the hands of an agent.

My salary was the princely sum of £4 per week, out of which I paid ten per cent to Mr. Earne, and five per cent to Zelia as I had promised.

....

[months later, on the eve of departing abroad on a 12-month tour...] I went to say goodbye to Zelia, and make the necessary arrangements to pay her, as we had agreed, five per cent of my salary. I suggested that I should send a postal order home every month during the period of the tour. Zelia looked blank. "Commission? What commission are you talking about?"

"The five per cent commission I agreed to pay you on any salary I earn in the theatre for the next ten years."

"I don't remember that," said Zelia. "I do remember accepting five per cent of your salary when you were in The Five O'Clock Girl, because you said you hadn't the cash to pay for the lessons."

"That's right" I said. "But I can remember the conversation clearly. 'In ten years' time,' you said, 'if you're lucky, that could amount to an awful lot of money. Do you think it's wise?' And I said, 'Of course I do.'"

Zelia smiled and said, "Johnny darling, of course I do remember. But I never had any intention of taking another penny from you after The Five O'Clock Girl closed. I told you at the time, if you remember, that Annie was my greatest friend. Do you really think I would seriously make a deal like that with her brother? Don't you realise you may, if you're lucky, be earning a great deal of money in a few years' time? Do you think I want a penny of it? What I do want is for you to go out on this tour, which is a great opportunity, work like a slave at your dancing, and if you make a success I should like to feel that perhaps I was responsible for a very small part of it. Believe me, that will be payment enough."

One never forgets the people who were kind and helpful when one was struggling up the first few rough steps of the ladder. Zelia Raye was one of them. I shall always be in her debt.

©*Sir John Mills 1980, 2001*

Up in the Clouds, Gentlemen Please was first published by Weidenfeld and Nicolson in 1980, then revised and reissued in 2001 by Orion Books

Robina Hinton

First may I explain how I came to be with Zelia: The Stage Branch examination was, in the 1930s, one exam only. The entrant was marked (not graded) and gained Elementary, Intermediate, or Advanced Pass, according to the mark obtained. There was a special acrobatic section, which was optional, and Modern Ballet.

Mary Archbutt entered three of us, her first entrants of this work. Joan Davis came up to Manchester to check the work and also to do our stage make-up.

After the exam I helped Mary Archbutt with her classes, which were taken both in the studio and outside. When I decided that the theatre would be better for me than teaching, Mary Archbutt advised me to go to Zelia Raye in London, which I did, but I remained a close friend of Mary Archbutt until she died.

The dance scene in London at that time was quite different from today. There was an enormous amount of work for chorus and soloists in shows, variety, cabaret and films and it was into this rich stream that Zelia pushed and advised us. It was possible to film during the day and do a floorshow at night. Salaries at that time were 3 pounds a week for chorus - soloists got quite a bit more.

The studio at 77 Dean Street took in the whole building except for the ground level. The main studio was on the first floor and the changing room was very inadequate. In hot weather there was always a bowl of ice-cubes for us to rub on heads and necks after class.

On the second floor was another studio, which was equipped with microphones and the version of video cameras and screen that we were taught to use; they were just coming into general use. The top floor was Zelia's personal flat and out of bounds to everyone. One room was laid out with electrical medical equipment, which she used on me once when I injured myself in class.

She once had a large cocktail party in the flat and we all waited on the famous people who were there.

Zelia had a ticket system for classes, which was available to those who were working. You bought a book of tickets which could be used at any time, signing one each time a class was attended. This meant that we were all able to keep in good practice.

Janet Cram was teaching at the studio, mostly tap, for which a "gramophone" was used. Zelia always said that it was better than a pianist, as it would not "give" in tempo.

Many famous people came to the limbering classes. Pamela Hulbert (Jack and Cecily's daughter) was there with a nanny, and wives of some of the leading film producers. It was to nanny or Janet that we fled in times of stress.

Zelia always took class with a long black stick. If you were lazy or careless she would use it to poke or sting the offending foot or leg. She was very insistent about our outdoor dress and behaviour. We always had to come to the studio looking what she called "West End smart," high heels, smart clothes, hats, gloves and a good facial make-up.

Her free sequences in class could be very difficult and, for the times, were far more advanced than were usually seen.

During the pantomime season Janet arranged the productions for Prince Littler and we were all shown a list of various venues for solo or chorus work available over the Xmas period so that we could have our choice before the public auditions.

We always understood that Zelia was Australian and came over here via the USA.

We also understood that for a period, Joan Davis was a partner in the studio, she often popped in and out before becoming ballet mistress at "the Lane" for Ivor Novello and Freddie Carpenter was also a close friend who came to the studio a great deal.

Zelia was a very private person and would never allow any of the students to breach the very firm teacher-pupil relationship; although we admired her work, she would not have wanted it.

1929 – a moment when Zelia was not hard at work on her soon-to-be-published first book, Rational Limbering

Gladys Dunlop

Headmistress, Wollongong, NSW Australia

Development of the creative in any art form is an absolute necessity for its own existence. Too readily we copy the forms that have sprung from the experience of other folk. In so doing, very often we suppress the very thing we are trying to develop.

For the past 27 years, dating back to the commencement of my own high school career, I have experienced and watched a development of dance in education.

Folk dancing is now enjoyed by most girls and a small percentage of boys. There has been some attempt at rhythmic work, better developed in the kindergarten classes, but it is quite true statement that 90% of the girls at twelve years of age have a very poor rhythmic sense, and only learn the dance after much practice in the steps and forms which seldom become spontaneous.

It was, indeed, a rare experience to meet Zelia Raye and to see her experiment with groups of children of all ages and types. The response in every case was spontaneous, the development, even with children of low intelligence, was free, and based on the child's own instinctive desire for rhythm and dance. The corelation of the dance form with the geometric form, and these in turn with the bodily movements, was stimulating, and gave much scope for a sound basis in both subjects. Time, rhythm and the forms of movement were woven into the dance while the child was still enjoying the experience, without tiring of the constant drill that so often must be the method. It was stimulating to see time, even syncopation, attacked joyously, then related to movement with hands or feet, and later developed into pattern.

With these basic things progressively developed, the dance becomes a natural form of expression, where the child can lose herself in the art form of her own creation.

Since meeting Miss Raye and discussing these matters with her, I have experienced a new joy in this subject. This year 1945, with girls of eight years, the co-relation of dance with music, geometry, history, geography and literature proved the efficacy of this method. After teaching a song, such as "White Birds" a ready response came from the best part of the class to create a suitable dance. The "fairies" and 'butterflies" in a recent operetta helped in the recreation of their own dances. It is only natural that these children desired to know something of the dance in the countries they studied.

One outstanding feature of the success of this method is the sense of achievement the child has, and the shy, retiring ones soon lose their sense of fear and await with joyous anticipation the opportunity for such expression. Another advantage of a system that develops this natural approach is that it is in line with modern educational methods in every way. The child must be the do-er, the child must create if his interest is to be sustained.

Recently I experimented with a group of girls who have been successful in their dancing examination. I asked such questions as: "Do two hops, two skips, and two jumps." The result was disastrous. In fact with few exceptions, these children fail where the untaught excel in this method. Being shown what to do often produces this type.

In conclusion, I would like to state that I look forward to the day when these thoughts are expressed in book form, that educators might consider them and give back to the people that which is their own heritage, "The Dance."

Published in Dance Journal 47, March 1951

Miss Raye's Visit to Australia

Dear Madam,

The Committee of the Theatrical Branch of the F.A.T.D. wishes me to inform you of their great appreciation of Miss Raye's work and efforts on behalf of your association while she was on holiday in Sydney.

Miss Raye's visit created much stimulation in the teachers of our Theatrical Branch, and all who came into contact with her were unanimous in their praise of her work and her charming personality.

I should like to add that Members of our Ballroom Branch who met Miss Raye heartily endorse the above comments of the Theatrical Branch Members.

With best wishes,

Yours faithfully,

Eileen Kane. (Organising Secretary)

Federal Association of Teachers of Dancing, Australia and New Zealand

Dance Journal, June 1952

Opposite – the ISTD holds a reception in the home of Doreen Austin to welcome Hanya Holm, choreographer of Kiss Me, Kate, and Hope Ryrie, president of the Federal Association of Australia and New Zealand.

Back row, l-r: Vivian Davies, Gen Sec of the ISTD, Mary Skeaping (Ballet Mistress, Sadler's Wells), Zelia Raye, Hope Ryrie, Ann Hutchinson (Director of the Dance Notation Bureau in New York), Eunice Weston (Melbourne), Olive Ripman, Murielle Ashcroft, Janet Cram, Victor Leopold.

Front Row: Anita Foster, Bert Stimmel, Doreen Austin, Marjorie Davies, Tom Parry, Joan Durrant, Mary Archbutt

Photo from Dance Journals 47, March 1951

Doris Humphrey

A personal letter to Zelia

Dear Zelia,

I think the book you have written is most comprehensive and sensible. You were so wise to include advice to the British dancers as to what to aim for, as I am sure [you] have always taken the broad view and therefore could lead young dancers to a successful career through really practical study. Of course I am especially impressed with your stress on meaning - we agree so well on this – it's a pleasure to see it said again and again until it finally prevails - as it must-.

I should love to see your work - also to work with the English dancers whom you have prepared so well. When you think the time is ripe for us to appear in England with our company we shall come.

Sincerely

Doris Humphrey

Zelia in Her Own Words

Published articles

Limbering And Stretching

Dancing Times December 1928 – Zelia Raye

A glimpse at the methods adopted in many American Schools of Dance, from whom have come those sensational dancers whose tours de force appeal to such a large section of the general public today, and who seem, of a consequence, to be able to command larger salaries and obtain more numerous engagements than the majority of their more conventionally trained sisters.

Let me start right away by saying that for some time I had it in mind to visit the States in order to study every kind of stage dancing over there. We are a conservative people, and, though I am a staunch little Britisher, I felt we had something to learn from our big, go-ahead cousins across the Atlantic. That this is so I discovered during the trip recently made to America.

"Progress! You've said it!" as they say over there. The method of stretching and limbering as practised in America is, I consider, one of the most important and beneficial methods of foundation technique. Most dance students know that limbering is the basis for every kind of dance work. It is necessary as grounding for operatic, acrobatic, and musical comedy dancing.

Barre work has been, and still is, the popular method over here to achieve the necessary results of suppleness and strength- the foundation of stage dancing.

Sometimes this method has another, and undesirable, result, namely that of producing unsightly leg muscles. In some schools in America the heavy part of the essential training is practised by

Opposite page – the School of Stage Dancing at 77 Dean St, London… "studio, lounge, writing and tea room, dressing rooms, showers, modern percussion and vibrator machines…"

the pupil flat on the floor, and by this simple expedient ugly muscles are given no chance to develop, and the student is able to get through much more work with far less fatigue.

The instructor is enabled to detect just where each individual pupil's weakness lies and train her accordingly.

Balance and strength come from the spine. Floor practice strengthens the spine without the student being aware of it. The good work goes swiftly on. Stretching, opening up, turning out - all is achieved in the minimum time, and with minimum expenditure of physical effort.

Do not imagine I am trying to sweep away barre and centre practice; I only wish to make clear the important point that the heaviest portion of a dancer's training can be made much lighter by the adoption of this floor method.

The operatic technique, which follows this, is very similar to our own teaching. American schools of dancing have adopted what is best in Italian, French and Russian methods, and do not limit themselves to any one system. I believe in this development of what might be called international technique - selecting the best from every method.

I have watched technique in Paris, Italy, Berlin, and during my stay in America I visited several studios in New York, Chicago, Los Angeles, etc., where I was very much impressed by the enthusiasm and ambition of the pupils, especially in schools catering for the stage. Then I discovered that while "art for art's sake" may be paramount, one very great incentive to work hard is the knowledge that remunerative engagements are waiting for those who are trained, or even partially trained. In Los Angeles, film producers often call upon a school of dancing to fill a dance scene, and such experience to the pupils during training is invaluable.

Most American girls have a natural talent for tempo and rhythm, so essential to a dancer. And this is not surprising since every American home is a jazz stronghold and America's

EXERCISE V.   FIG. 5.

Stand erect with the head upright, the knees straight, feet together and arms stretched forward in a line with the shoulders, the palms downwards.

1. Bend the knees until the body is in a sitting position, keeping the legs together and heels on the ground (see Fig. 5).

2. Pass the arms backwards.

3, 4. Turn the palms facing upwards and, keeping the arms fully stretched and tense, return to upright position with a restrained upward swing of the arms. This should be done as though the arms were supporting a weight.

Perform this exercise several times.

Note.—This exercise stretches the lower tendons at the back of the legs.

daughters are brought up on syncopated rhythm. Students taking up dancing professionally usually study ballet, musical comedy, acrobatic, character and buck dancing, and a teacher can very quickly advise as to which style they should specialize. One very important part of the training is "showmanship" meaning the development of the individuality, which gives expression to every movement. Personality, style, elevation, eyes, arms, smile, deportment: these are what bring a girl out of the chorus, out of team work and make her one by herself, a finished artist. In America, as over here, a girl with knowledge of ballet dancing only, finds it difficult to secure engagements. On the other hand there is a great demand for the accomplished all-round dancer, with a knowledge of the technique of ballet, both as a principal and for teamwork.

In the *Ziegfield Follies*, and in *Rio Rita* in New York, the Albertina Rasch dancers from the Albertina Rasch School, are creating quite a sensation. These girls specialise in troupe work "on the pointe" and their rhythm precision, faultless technique, and perfect teamwork appeal greatly to their audiences. The girls also have the opportunity for individual work in very charming ballets.

The Dancing Masters of America Incorporated hold what is called an annual Normal School and Convention in New York, for dancing teachers, professionals and students. It lasts over four weeks, during which seven hours' instruction is given daily to pupils in ballet, musical comedy, step dancing, Oriental, Spanish, acrobatic and ballroom dancing. The instructors are leading teachers and professionals, specialising in these different branches. This scheme would, I think, be very valuable to many of our dancers, who at present are finding considerable difficulty in obtaining this kind of tuition with the idea of obtaining engagements later on, and they would be more certain of a remunerative return if such an annual school were possible over here.

In America, schools which commercialise dancing are very well patronised by those taking up dancing as a career. These schools are often linked up with a theatre which to my mind is ideal, while other schools, the aim of which may be "higher art," usually have their own ballets and companies in which pupils obtain engagements, but it is doubtful if the individual pupil could compete successfully in the open market with the product of the former schools, as the theatrical demand is obviously not for that style of dancing alone.

Modern Spectacular Dancing - Some Random Notes

The Dancing Times December 1928

I believe most dancers now realize that whatever branch of dancing they take up, if they specialize at all, one of their biggest assets is to have perfect muscular control.

The staunch supporters of Grecian dancing will agree that ballet and acrobatic dancing are both artificial, and when I say "artificial" I merely mean to imply that pointe work and back bends etc., etc., are not natural movements of the body. Exponents of one should not criticize the other. I am a supporter of operatic dancing, but I realize its limitations.

Good acrobatic and adagio dancers include operatic work in their training, and therefore have an advantage over the more conservative ballet-trained workers.

The combination of acrobatic training, together with stretching and limbering, and operatic is gradually finding favour with our artists and teachers.

Early training of the body is vastly important. To misquote an old saying, the technically perfect dancer is not born but made! The artist works at perfection gradually, but as training goes nowadays it is not work, but pleasure, bringing the sheer joy of physical fitness.

Giving Auditions

Girls giving audition numbers usually remember that the splits is always an effective movement, but this alone does not make dancers of them. They must also realise that trained strength in the abdominal muscles is necessary for any high kicking. It is true that in some instances the practice of the splits may be outside the student's power, but it must be recognized that in the majority of cases this exercise is merely part of the necessary training for all high kicking.

Have Lovely Legs

There is a great demand at the present time for buck and rhythm dancing, and a number of dancers are unsuccessful at auditions because of their ignorance of this branch of the work. The old fashioned idea that buck dancing spoilt operatic work is now exploded. In actual fact the contrary is the case, and after a strenuous ballet lesson buck dancing relaxes the muscles and prevents the hardening, and tightening up, from which so many ballet dancers suffer.

Make Dancing Pay

Now do not us lose sight of the fact that it is possible for a dancer to have marvellous technique and very little else. Dancers themselves are too much inclined to concentrate on the physical side of dancing, forgetting the importance of the mental and poetical, one might say the spiritual, side of their art.

This is a great pity. The really beautiful dancer must be impressionable, receptive. Moreover, the poetical keeps pace with the practical, inasmuch as it is not the dancer who boasts an amazing technique who draws a big public-and a big salary! It is the artist who, to borrow a word from Eleanor Glyn, has "It" and technique combined.

I think it is not too sweeping to say that all dancers are artificial, and therefore less attractive as they might be, until they succeed in expressing personality. In these days, when we view dance more or less theatrically, and from the angle of superficial decorative movement, it is not always easy for individuality to break through. Only the true artist will triumph and give dance vital creations. "And this reminds me of what I consider is one of the greatest handicaps to English dancers. They do not lack personality, but have a dreadful self-consciousness, which hinders their technical development almost as much as it impairs their powers of self expression.

The old school of dancing used pantomime in an artificial and stilted manner, but just as the old school of acting has changed so has gesture and mime. It is the day of realities. Without feeling dance is meaningless.

Dancing Times: "a new picture of Miss Joan Davis of the Zelia Raye School and ballet mistress at Drury Lane who has been producing and appearing in cabaret at the "Tricity" Restaurant with her own troupe."

The Art Of Doris Humphrey

The Dancing Times November 1931 - An Appreciation by Zelia Raye and Joan Davis

Miss Doris Humphrey and Mr. Charles Weidman are products of the "Denishawn School" and their work is exercising a great influence among the "concert artists" of New York.

To be quite honest, what interested us most in the dance world of America was undoubtedly the work of Doris Humphrey and Charles Weidman. Here we have two people who are certainly offering the dance world something entirely new. With their concert group they have toured from Coast to Coast in America. It is to be hoped they will soon be seen in England. The name that Miss Humphrey is carving for herself in the history of Dance is due to the originality of her conceptions and the dexterity with which she and her group fulfil these to the last word. The "Life of the Bee" is one of her best-known earlier works. This is performed unaccompanied except for a droning chorus off stage which comes in occasionally to intensify the story.

"The Water Study" as a title struck us as rather ambitious, but when we saw it carried out unaccompanied by Miss Humphrey's group, we realised that an idea born in her head is only the first step, which in this case was carried right to the very lapping of the waves on the beach. To show how this study impressed others, we quote below from the New York Times.

"In this choreography, Miss Humphrey has pictured water in its every flow from the slow swell and ripple to the breaking high waves of foam. "So exactly was the representation in the co-operative body movement that it was wonderful in its analogy. The wave beat seem to give it sufficient rhythm to suggest design beyond the mere imitation of Nature and the result was a thing of dramatic beauty"

Miss Humphrey's latest achievement is the "Dance of the Chosen", the theme of which is based on an old American religious sect called the Shakers.

"God hath revealed that eternal life shall be the reward of those who are shaken clean of sin" - old Shaker journal. This is

Dancing Times used this photo of Zelia above this article

accompanied by a drum, accordion and voice, and it is most impressive.

There is neither time nor space to mention all the works these two artists and their group perform, covering as it does a very varied field of work, for which they use either symphony orchestra, piano, voice or no accompaniment at all. In all cases the theme is the one important point. Miss Humphrey explains it thus:

"The dance is the thing, not the costumes, decorations, music, or drama. Therefore costumes are only brief suggestions, unless some heavy ornamentation or length of train is an integral part of the dance conception. Decoration is never an end in itself, and stage appurtenances are reduced to the minimum. Music is for tone, colour and rhythm and stimulation to the dancer - but we can also dance quite well by our inner emotional rhythm or by the dynamics of natural forces.

"Our dances cover a wide range from the classic 'Air for the G String' to the 'Drama of Motion' which is modern in the sense of being free from the other arts - but the keynote to them all is the intensification of the dance subordination of externals."

The aim of Miss Humphrey and Mr. Weidman is not only to teach and use their group but also to make each member a creator. As a result a small contingency of the big group have started what is known in the concert world as the "Little Group." Watching a dress rehearsal in the studio, we were amazed to learn that the compositions executed were their own. It was easy to see how delighted Miss Humphrey was to watch her artistes painting with their own brushes. The work of Miss Humphrey and Mr. Weidman whether solo, duet or group, though distinctly individual, always blends and harmonises, one the compliment to the other.

The unselfishness of such work, and the creative power at the back of it, is bound to spread its influence to the far corners of the world.

Round The Dancing Schools Of New York

The Dancing Times December 1931 - Zelia Raye and Joan Davis

To give a detailed description of all we did and saw in America would take a whole book in itself, so we'll just take a quick trip round.

Starting with our first Sunday in New York, we were guests at the Dancers' Club, where they were holding a welcome home tea for Mr. Ted Shawn, who gave a chat on his tour and impressions of Europe. At the Sunday teas the aim is to have someone with anything of special interest to talk on it to members. One of these was devoted to the showing of our African War Dance film and talk which we gave on things general.

We made the acquaintance of many teachers, all of whom were very charming and hospitable, welcoming us to several of their dance conferences, which we found very interesting.

Owing to the opportunities America has to offer both artistically and financially, it has gathered under its wing an amazing group of teachers of every conceivable style of dancing. Most of the studios are very spacious and attractive, and those which Mr. Louis Chalif has built for himself in New York actually border on the palatial. There are two huge ballrooms, a roof studio, and a most attractive, cool and quiet vestibule, which stands on guard between the noise of the streets and the peaceful atmosphere for study which pervades the whole building. In these studios we watched Mr. Angel Cansino give a very interesting class in Spanish dancing, and Mr. Yakovleff, an inspired ballet class, giving so much of the art as well as the technique of dancing. The season for Mr. Chalif's classes had not yet started, as he was busy with summer congress work.

A few blocks away, Mr. Gluck-Sandor has his intimate Theatre Studio. Here he has made ingenious use of the very limited space, having turned one end of the studio into an unraised stage by a framework of curtains. The scenery, painted by well-known American artists, gives a very clever illusion of space. The lighting is effectively produced by overhead lamps and limes. The other half of the studio is built up in a series of wide steps to the ceiling, each of which is lettered like the stalls in the theatre. These can accommodate about one hundred people. The dressing rooms are under the steps so there is no waste of space. The rest of the premises consist of a reception room and offices.

Under the heading of the dance centre, Mr. Sandor's aim is to build up a permanent dance theatre. The first ballet of the season, which opened on August 28th, was a modern version of "Petrouchka", direction and choreography by Gluck-Sandor. The season will consist of six ballets varying from reviews of those made famous by Diaghilev and some never before presented in America. The theatre will also be let to dance artists wishing to give recitals at a rate so reasonable that there will be an opportunity for them to make a profit. Apart from his activities for the dance centre, Mr. Sandor is also responsible for two ballets in Earl Carroll's "Vanities" at the new Earl Caroll Theatre.

The Albertina Rasch studios were a hive of industry, and the fact that her girls are in such demand seems to inspire the students of her school to hurry to that stage of perfection, which makes groups of her dancers in various New York shows so very successful.

Certainly circumstances in America (mainly the size of the country) offer girls a bigger chance of employment after training. The Chester Hale School has always as big a demand as it can supply. Mr. Hale has a permanent unit (team) at the Capitol Theatre, New York, with which he designs and produces each week an attractive presentation on a most extravagant scale, and it is a very common thing for him to have twenty other units on the road at the same time. All this has been accomplished in a comparatively short time. The girls work very hard and are in the theatre all day, but the pay is excellent and they don't seem to mind at all. As a matter of fact, at dress rehearsal which we went to see at 8am, they were full of pep which often lasts them for sixteen hours a day.

Mr. Jack Manning, a well-known dance producer in New York, has a very successful school just off Broadway from which there continually flows talent which quickly finds its way to the front.

An outstanding example of this is of a young usher at the Palace theatre, New York, who trained with Mr. Manning in his spare time, and eventually got his chance to make an appearance, making a terrific overnight success at the theatre where only a short time before he had been showing people their seats.

Then there are the Billy Pierce studios, the fame of which has already spread to London owing to the success that he and Mr. Buddy Bradley have made of the productions they have done in this country. Here you have a coloured teaching staff, and all the ingenious tap rhythm steps with which the black American seems to overflow.

Rhythm with the feet - strumming on the ukulele or a few blue chords on the piano – you can't leave an atmosphere like this without getting something, that something which makes tap dancing so much nearer the artistic than one can imagine possible.

Mr. Fred Le Quorn specializes in exhibition ballroom dancing, and he has to his credit a considerable number of well-known acts produced by him in the various shows and cabarets. He is mainly responsible for spreading the popularity of dances such as Rumba, Tango, and original Cuban dances. With Miss Ann Pennington he demonstrated and originated a novelty dance number known as "The Pepper Shaker." A Fox Movietone was taken of this as a jazz variation of a Fox-trot.

Several teachers who met Miss Lucille Stoddart a few years ago, when she demonstrated for the Imperial Society, will be pleased to know that her big venture of organizing an all-star Teacher's Course at the Hotel Astor, New York, was a huge success. Everything that a teacher could possibly want to know was included as, apart from the different styles of dancing, there were lectures on the business and advertising side of our profession and many other of the little side issues which go towards the making of a successful dancing school.

To mention just a few of the names, which will be familiar on this side, there were Fowler and Tamara, who it will be remembered were in one of Mr. Cochran's productions at the London Pavilion. Bill Robinson, that inimitable "Rhythm Daddy" Harland Dickson, Mr. Tarasoff, Gluck-Sandor, Nimura. These names alone give one a very good idea of the vast range of work that was covered. Miss Stoddart is already deep in the throes of preparing her 1932 Summer Course, which looks like living up to the standard that she has set for herself this year.

We cannot close this article without telling you of the wonderful ballet presented by Miss Ruth St. Denis during the three days' concert programme, which she and Mr. Ted Shawn, with the Denishawn dancers, gave at the Lewisohn Stadium. This vast concert auditorium with the starlit sky for a roof, holding 20,000 people, and with the symphony orchestra under the direction of Hans Lange, was the most fitting background for the inspired and inspiring work of Miss St. Denis's "The Prophetess," an allegorical dance drama to the music of Mars from "The Planets" (Holst) and "Holy, Holy, Holy" (Dyke), Miss St Denis herself taking part of the prophetess. As well as students from her own school, she used a number of young men from Mr. Henry Powers Technical Rhythm Dancers from the West Side Y.M.C.A. The following from the programme notes will give a better idea than we could of the story.

"'The Prophetess' is a symbolical study in mass movement of the opposing forces of humanity. On the one hand, those elements of drudgery, diversity and war, which bespeak the materialistic viewpoint of life; on the other hand, the harmonious unity arising from a revelation of the spiritual conception of the universe and symbolized in the Prophetess, as danced by Miss St. Denis.

"The Prophetess is seen seated upon the Mount of Vision; she beholds the endless round of humanity; and its antagonisms culminating in war. The figure of the Prophetess is the symbol of Man's ideal of unity, harmony, and power. She is swayed, through her sympathy, by the cataclysm, which breaks before her, and descending to serve the race, is caught between the opposing forces and temporarily defeated. In the hour of defeat, the light of Spiritual Vision appears to her. The path of her soul's progress is through the oppressing and opposing forces of her own being. Through desire and fear she slowly struggles to attain the Summit of Illumination. Here, wrapped in the divine light, she experiences the Cosmic Consciousness, the realisation of the Unity of Life. Through harmonious rhythm she symbolizes this Cosmic Consciousness and transmits it to humanity below. As the new rhythm takes hold of the lives of Men, they are lifted out of their agony of confusion and enter into the Divine Rhythm, breaking forth into an ecstatic paean. The preliminary rhythm is intended as a symbol of the rhythm of humanity in its work and play."

Let The Films Help You To Remember.

The Dancing Times December 1931 - Zelia Raye and Joan Davis

If you take your own moving pictures you will find the initial expenditure repaid a thousand fold.

W e have been asked to write an article on what we think will be the advantages of the moving picture camera to the dancing world. Well! We feel that as dancing is the art of movement it is only natural that it should gain from a co-operation with the moving picture, and the idea of utilising this for making dance records both at home and abroad has interested us for a long time.

Our real basic plans for putting this into action were not completed until after our experiment of filming the war dances of South Africa. The useful knowledge that this brought to all who saw it made us finally decide to get these ideas into working order. On showing this film to teachers and others interested in dance, both in England and in America there was unanimous

Zelia, left, and Joan ...practicing as they preached

feeling that an international exchange of dance films was going to shed a strong and helpful ray of light on dancing all over the world.

America has already foreseen this and Dr. Coomeraswamy, Keeper of Indian and Mohammedan Art in the Boston Museum, who is also an authority on Oriental dance and drama, has an interesting library of films of native dances of India, Cambodia and Ceylon. There are several enterprising concerns going out from America to the far corners of the world making sound films of the various tribal and native dances. Meantime with the facilities for home moving picture photography being brought within the means and capabilities of the amateur, we foresee a great opportunity for recording work, which should be a far superior and certainly more interesting form of compiling dance notes.

Mr. Tarasoff, a well-known teacher in New York, has already made experiments in this direction. While we were here he entertained us with charming hospitality showing us his very interesting films and discussing with us the advantages that he had already found in locating with the cruel and penetrating eye of the slow motion camera the strong and weak points of his different pupils, and the greater advantages to come when picture records of the notable works of great artists would be made, enabling us to pass down to the coming generations what we have learned in our time.

What a priceless treasure a few films of that beloved artist, Pavlova, would be to us now, and the beautiful ballets that Diaghilev brought to these shores.

Although we look to the natives for the authentic national dances, it is often necessary in musical presentations etc. to give a general effect of dances from other countries. This is where the producer and teacher should find the film a great asset in giving them the outline of various themes, which should result in their getting a more convincing atmosphere. There are many dances, which we have never seen, and many more we have not even heard of, and it is encouraging to know that journeys are being made to the ends of the earth in order to collect these original records. Films such as these should stimulate our inventive brains and prevent us from getting fanatical over the so-called new methods when we see in the primitive so much modern work.

In this age of invention when we feel ourselves so advanced it is interesting to think that lost in the maze of education and technique we are now groping for our real selves. Let us realise that it is ourselves we are seeking, not any particular method and apply this awakening to the work we already know. It is to be hoped that all those who have interesting films of dancing will make it known so that in this way an exchange system could be organised as we feel that apart from their instructive value, this would act as an international link bridging the difficulties of the cost and time of travelling which have hitherto kept us apart.

Speaking from our own personal experience, we know we could never have kept an accurate picture of the work and knowledge of the steps, etc., that we got in America, from memory and dance notes, but by taking films of the various teachers and ourselves at the time, we now just throw these onto the screen and in a few minutes have refreshed our memories, and in quite an entertaining way too.

We look forward in future to keeping up to date through this medium. We can see a time not far distant when a 16mm projector for showing home 'movie' films will be part of the equipment of every studio so that even those who are not interested in the taking of films will be able to avail themselves of those in the film renting libraries. The projectors are now very easy to operate. Those who wish to take films will be glad to know that wonderful results can now be got in indoor work by using two 500-watt lamps and the new super-sensitive film. In the summer, of course, the garden makes a delightful setting.

Our aim is to start a centre for dance films in London in the very near future, and we would be glad to help anyone interested.

The Essentials of Dancing

The Dance Journal, June 1933 - Zelia Raye and Joan Davis

Dancing is the natural expression of emotion. As an art, it is the educated state of natural impulses, and it should not be neglected as a means of development in education.

There can, of course, be no final technique in dancing any more than in other arts and sciences as long as we remain creative. There are, however, basic fundamentals, which would help if applied to the individual need.

A dancer must be strong enough physically to execute the dance so that the emotions can be used to express the theme. An exhausted body has no strength to convey anything but physical effort. Therefore the first essential is to be fit.

Limbering and stretching exercises have been, and still are, being exploited to perfect the physical condition of the dancer. If an exercise is for stretching, then this must be done to the utmost limit. Some students do not realise this, but they could be helped if given an object to stretch to, when their own imagination is not enough. Gradually this will awaken their own vitality and force. Once the imagination is aroused and the quality of values realised, the dancer will apply soft or hard lines to the movement as required.

It is necessary to have a definite personality for the stage world, and this is not possible without definite action and mental thought. The art of movement, too, has to be well considered. What we call "stage sense" must be acquired and developed so that the dancer may not be so cramped on a large stage that she looks insignificant, or so broad that she cannot confine herself to a limited space. The picture must fit the frame.

It is necessary that the student should know the full quality of different tempi. First she must dance to time - but it must not end here. The antidote to the monotony of time is "rhythm," which is the implement with which we colour the dance. Rhythm is a force of nature and, as such, cannot be ignored if the dancer is to get a harmonious and vital effect. It is the expression of the individuals timing, and when one realises that there are nearly four hundred organs of the body that work rhythmically, then one should recognise and pay more attention to it as an educational force. One cannot ignore the fact that some people react better to quick rhythm while others respond more readily to slow. This very "timing" is part of the individual character.

While it is well to nurse to some extent the individual's rhythm, it is also necessary in some cases to blend the opposition so that one can counter-balance what might be excessive calm or excitability. This penetrates deeper than mere dancing. It is an understanding of human nature. Having trained the body physically and the nerves and mentality to work in co-ordination with the physical movement, the student is ready to develop on any lines of dancing, and is well balanced for any profession or mode of life.

What Is Stage Dancing?

South African Dancing Times – Zelia Raye.

This can be answered in a few words. Stage Dancing is dancing of any description served up in such a way that the public at large could appreciate and understand it. In other words it is marketable. This will not destroy the art of the dance but will breed in it a generous portrayal that all will understand.

No country or capital can provide enough recitals to keep a great number of dancers employed, and it is only a few artistes who have the business capacity to exploit their own work. Therefore, if dancers want to make a profession of the art, they must consider what is wanted.

Many teachers are now realising that they must use their discrimination on the most direct method of teaching the dance to the young idea. In this teaching Rhythm is an essential. It is the very feeling of the dance, the atmosphere that gives it life and vitality. In primitive races one sees what a terrific and natural force Rhythm is within us. Civilisation and mechanical movement have to a great extent deadened this natural expression, and the sooner it is rekindled the better it will be for the education of the dancer, and the physical well-being of humanity in general. Nowadays children are sent for dancing lessons as part of their education and in many cases have no feeling for dancing or rhythm. This is a point that teachers would do well to pay more attention to, the instilling of a sense of rhythm, as it is vital in the dancers training and we cannot afford to ignore it.

The training of students should be placed in the following rotation, to make it easier for teachers and pupils.

Stretching And Limbering to make the body a fit vehicle for dance. We must not forget that dancing is the art of movement. Limbering and stretching only prepare the body and act as a foundation technique.

Rhythmical Training: the value of different tempos. Rhythm is the quality which relieves the monotony of ordinary tempo. The combination of Limbering and Rhythm should produce a harmonious working of mind and body together, and fit the student to advance in the art in general. In group and line work spacing of steps should be considered and the dancer should be able to broaden or limit the style as required in the case of characterisation or stage spacing.

The Tap Technique as used by the Stage Branch of the ISTD has been compiled to simplify the teaching of Tap dancing, which, apart from its popularity, is proving a very successful method of teaching rhythm.

Limbering and Stretching, Side and Centre Practice, Tap Technique, Kicks and Acrobatics do not make an attractive show for the shop window. Technique alone is not enough.

Production should go along with the training. The art of Production is the "salesman" of the work. The teacher should be able to produce a dancer; a dancer an entertainment. In this, of course, there is much to be taken into account in addition to the actual routine, such as suitable costuming, grooming, make up etc., which play a great party in the success or otherwise of the performer. There will always be those who specialise in this, as in other arts, but for the majority a sound all round training fits them best for the theatrical and the teaching professions

The Stage Branch of the ISTD has now three grades of children's examinations that are proving very helpful. Negotiations are also in progress for holding Children's Examinations in South Africa, and as there are several members of the Stage Branch now teaching in South Africa who are very enthusiastic this should not be very difficult to organise.

The technique of analysing in detail spontaneous rhythmic movement is not easy, and it is due to the ceaseless effort of those who analyse movement that we now have various skilled techniques in the field of dance and sport: in dance-skill for the sake of form, and in sport-form for the sake of skill. This physical technique, supplemented by the correct timing, gives the form of the movement, but there is a difference. For instance one individual may have it rhythmically, one not so rhythmically, and a third without any rhythm at all.

Any of my readers who are interested in sport should have no

More Bertha Reid than Zelia Raye: not yet the finished article

difficulty in recognising the three classes, and even those unacquainted with sport will admire rhythmical movement without being able to say why. So it is with dancing. A large percentage of an audience can look at a dancer without knowing anything about technique or rhythm and still be appreciative of the combination of the perfect exponent.

Now many teachers have emphasised form to the detriment of the individual's training as a whole. It is, however, only when there is a balance of the abstract qualities - thought and feeling, which make the content of the dance - that we recognise personality. Do not confuse this with theatrical "top show" which is very different from an intelligent understanding of dance.

The dance may be simple or complex, but it can only appeal to the onlooker if the dance expresses the joy of movement. I should therefore advise all teachers to stress first of all the importance of health and happiness. A happy child will learn much quicker than an unhappy one. Do not force the technique, but let the growing child experience the joy of doing the familiar thing well. We aim to train, not strain.

On the other hand, if the pupil is held back or is merely imitating when she has really the intelligence to understand and grasp the technique, it is not uncommon to find boredom setting in, which is often mistaken for laziness. This we must at all costs try to prevent, for, as we all know, boredom kills the love of dance.

As our Branch covers such a wide field, let us bear in mind that it is only by a broad outlook and vision that we can build up the further development which should be our aim.

The Interdependence Of Technique, Rhythm and Expression

Dance Journal, 1935 – Zelia Raye

No matter how vivid the imagination may be, the artiste is powerless thereto except through the medium of technique. If technique is ignored, only the ugly and uncontrolled movements can be portrayed.

In primitive races the dance was the natural human reaction to rhythmic sound such as the beat of the tom-tom, and from this follows in the course of progress that beautiful music should mean the greater development of the dance, if the music is understood and its form and rhythm intelligently grasped. The lack of this understanding has resulted in the lack of co-ordination of mind and body, for if one cannot *feel* the music, one cannot express it. Therefore may I say that the reaction to primitive music, which is very noticeable in many modern techniques, may in itself be a step in the right direction, if it creates a feeling for expression of rhythm in our modern compositions. We believe that rhythm and an understanding of music should play an important part in a child's training, so that a well-balanced mind and body may ensure freedom of thought and movement in the dance.

Every new method of dancing is open to criticism, but I should be the last to say that any method is without benefit to dancing in general.

We in the Stage Branch call for a definite standard of rhythm and physical development, but it cannot be too strongly emphasized that the training of the student does not finish with the achievement of correct technique. Here is the trap into which so many fall, the idea that technique of itself is the aim and object to be attained, thus restricting the development of those qualities, which are so essential to the finished artiste.

In the world of dance today, we have on the one hand those who concentrate on technique to the exclusion of everything else, and, on the other, those who repudiate every accepted form of technique and then set out to achieve harmonious and rhythmical movement with an ungoverned and uncontrolled body.

But the fact remains that a knowledge of technique in the dance, as in every other art, is the only foundation upon which to build: without it one has no medium through which to express one's ideas and is hopelessly restricted in bodily range of movement.

In the recent syllabi of the Children's Examinations of the Stage Branch, this physical and rhythmical training is insisted upon. The child must know as much as is in the syllabus, but high marks are only obtained by good execution.

These grades have been compiled with the idea of attaining a standard of work, but give ample scope for the teacher to develop originality, as it is our intention that the teacher should develop through this method the theory of composition, just as the propositions in Euclid are intended to develop the reasoning powers of the individual. It is very interesting to make up exercises and gradually develop them into dance movement.

Good deportment is essential. This has been rather neglected by dancers and more attention should be paid to it. Children should be taught to walk to music - change to the ball of the foot and change to running. A decided slowing down of rhythm should be noticeable between running and walking again. These exercises should be given to various rhythms.

The following ideas may be useful in showing how to create the dance feeling:

1. Start with elementary rhythms and gradually advance to more complicated ones.

2. Add movement to make the pattern of the dance. Movement of the legs, body and arms.

3. Cultivate a sense of direction and concentration.

The simplest movement can then be made quite beautiful.

Joan Davis – long-time partner and collaborator of Zelia; later she opened her own school. Joan was a regular performer herself, a producer at Drury Lane and the Hippodrome, including No No Nannette; she choreographed the dances in the Harry Roy film Royal Romance ...

The Composition Of Dances Based On The Tap Technique

Dance Journal, June 1936 Zelia Raye

To be a good composer of tap routines, it is essential to have a fine sense of time and rhythm, that is, a feeling for what one might call the heart beat of the music. I have noticed that if a teacher composes an exercise from the tap technique, without this feeling for rhythm, the response from the pupil will be slow and uninteresting. Tap dancing is happy and frivolous, and to remove that feeling is to remove the reason for tap dancing. Anyone who unconsciously taps the foot rhythmically when they hear music has that feeling. I should advise teachers to study good rhythm tap steps and fit them to different tempi of music. Sometimes a slow step can be executed quicker, and a quick one, slower, but there must not be a feeling of agitation or dragging. If you can do this, you will soon be able to discriminate as to the best type of step to fit the music. If one has perfect co-ordination of mind and body, the body will respond quickly to the mind, but not so simple in practice.

There are lots of people who find tap dancing fairly easy. They can let themselves go, and consequently pick it up very quickly. On the other hand, there are those who find it difficult to relax, and by being too serious, tense themselves and, by their lack of feeling, make their own obstacle to success. I think it helpful to hum the rhythm of the step while dancing. This will make breathing more rhythmical and help to avoid this tenseness.

The more we know of tap dancing the more we can appreciate good work. It is wonderful the high standard some dances have, and are attaining. We teachers are interested in simplifying the teaching of these intricate steps to the would-be tap dancer. Our system of technique is already proving its value, but we must realize the danger of what is just technique and not stop there. That does not make the dancer who holds our interest and makes tap dancing a joy to watch. It is the dancer with perfect rhythm.

After all if one has perfect rhythm one has personality. As one progresses in the technique, much more attention must be paid to this. I often say that the elementary stage in modern tap is the footwork, and one progresses to the advanced stage when the whole body is alive to movement, otherwise one develops an old-fashioned style. Easy movement of the legs; snake hips; Rumba style; are all part of the modern movement.

One might compare the execution and composition of tap with the execution and composition of music. The theory of tap, like the theory of music, is a sure foundation technique. It does not guarantee the secret of success, but it is constructive and will lead to the road of success.

The teacher or dancer, however, who simply learns the steps without this knowledge of theory, might execute those steps well, but will be limited as to how to construct and compose a dance. The artist with inspiration and innate rhythm will always be the exception to this. I have learned some marvellous steps from such artists who could not analyse their work. It is usually difficult to pick up the steps this way, but on analysing these same steps by the method we now use in the Stage Branch I have found that I have been able to get quick results. I have also taught this method to excellent dancers, who realize the value of having a definite method of teaching. It is quite possible that through this method a teacher might be a good composer without being a good performer, just as we have many composers of music who lack the brilliance of a performer, and vice versa.

As an aid to the understanding of tap composition, might I suggest that it is wise to have the music played well or to get a little inspiration by hearing it played on a good record; start beating rhythmically until you understand the tempo; then take the first eight bars and think out a good rhythm. Tap this rhythm on the table with a pencil and add the count to it, for instance;

&8, &a1, &2, &3, &4, &5&a6, 7, &8.

Now add from the glossary what you think would be suitable steps for this timing and you may find you have thought out quite a good step. The next step must start on the count of 1, as you will notice you finish the first step on 8, and if you make the second step on 7 you can repeat these two steps and that will take eight bars of music. When you have fixed the step, think of the pattern and direction, the style, the showmanship and feeling; this will give you an idea of how to construct a routine. For the beginner I always advise learning good steps and practice until one can execute them with satisfaction to oneself and others. Do not bore people with your own compositions, although it is wise to try them. You will soon realize if you are creating interest. I think we all know how a good pianist can sell a popular melody; so it is with tap, it is the performer who can put it over every time, even the simplest step. We none of us can lay down hard and fast rules. The results of teaching depend a great deal on the style and personality of the teacher.

Some teachers expect their pupils to learn by sight, others by technique, and again by rhythm and technique, etc. You have the choice of which of these standards you wish to attain, and you can only advise by your own experience and with the idea of helping those who wish our advice.

In modern dance production there is a great mixing of techniques, and, for the successful stage dancer I maintain that a knowledge of tap, musical comedy, and ballet is essential. Only the other day I required some girls to dance a tap routine with boys in a film production, but those routines are no longer just tap, they are a combination of different styles, and I mention this for the guidance of teachers.

Basic Rhythms and Pattern And Direction

Bulletin 33 September 1947 – Zelia Raye

I should like to draw attention to the fact that it is just twenty years since I first started to interest the ISTD in my approach to Dance. That was in 1927, when I was invited to give a lesson to the members; and that is why I have chosen for my first subject today the same type of lesson - basic rhythms. I have been told I have a dialectical approach to Dance, but I also recognise the value of the imitative method for quicker results.

The subject of "music and movement" is the approach of the musician to movement. My method of "movement and music" is the approach of the dancer to music. There is a difference. Both music and dance can be independent of each other, but when amalgamated must be related. The dancer can give inspiration to the creative musician, but we must be grateful to the musician for keeping alive the various dance rhythms that have been created. There will be no contradiction on "basic rhythms" in either approach. If this relationship of movement and music is not understood or missed out - as it has been in so many dancers' training - the dance will lack the strong growth that good roots give. I am aware that the creative artist must always be allowed the freedom to add fresh values to their chosen art. I am trying to keep the development of the teaching of Dance simple and balanced.

This subject of basic rhythm must be approached with an open mind free from set techniques. It is in this subject that dance, as an Art form, will develop and differs from the Art of Dancing which, in my opinion, is the difference between learning dancing and learning skilled techniques and dances.

I have endeavoured to write out a more detailed Syllabus for the Children's Grades. I find, however, that in the examinations too many candidates lack the feeling of the simplest rhythms, which are instinctive in the child. I should like, therefore, to explain the pitfalls in this Grade; for instance, after mastering the balance of walking the child prefers to skip. If "hop step" is taught technically before the instinctive imitative movement has been developed, it retards progress as the accent is very often changed from "&1 to "1&." "Hop step" to rhythm is similar to a Hopi Indian step. This is a very important point, and if not understood by the teacher this rhythmical difference will cause confusion later on. An ordinary walking rhythm to 4/4 time is instinctive, but by adding the discipline of time-slow, medium, quick, plus missed beats, accented beats, added beats- one can rediscover dance rhythms and create interesting rhythms and patterns.

There seems to be some confusion as to what is meant by the time of the piece, and the following explanation might be helpful.

"It is used in two ways: first, to refer to the speed or tempo of the music as usually indicated at the beginning; second, to refer to the number and value of the notes employed as a unit in each measure (or their equivalent) as indicated by the time signature placed at the beginning directly after the key signature."

What I am now stressing is the importance of bringing out and developing rhythm rather than pushing it in. If we could strike a balance I am sure that by forming groups for experimental production we should improve the quality of the work.

Another heading exquisitely illustrated for American Tap Dancing

The Common Sense Of Dance

Dance Journal, 39 March 1949 - Zelia Raye

What we dance, how, and why, are questions one must strive to answer for oneself. It is really a matter of taste, environment and opportunity.

The standard of Stage Dancing depends on the dictates of taste and fashion, therefore an educated audience is equally important in improving the taste and standard. We as teachers should be the first to recognise the changes that are taking place so that we can live up to the aims of the Branch, i.e., "to develop and maintain a high standard of modern Stage dancing." If a subject is to be taught correctly, the method should have the same basic fundamentals, whether for amateur or professional use. The future dance audience would then be created at the same time as the dancer who has a natural ability, excels in the work, and decides to make it a career. As the percentage of dancers going onto the Stage is very small in comparison with the numbers who train, we as teachers are not going to find satisfaction in our work if we only create frustrated dancers. If, however the pupil benefits physically and mentally and is given an appreciation of dance, then our subject can be very important.

The Stage Branch syllabus is really based on the Common Sense of Dance. The whys and wherefores should always arouse curiosity. To impart with knowledge the impetus to think, to stimulate the pupil's mind so that what has been learned is understood and not merely memorised, should be the aim of the teacher.

Children should first be taught to love dancing so that the spirit of dance is kept alive, then the formal training is more easily accepted without sacrificing the feeling. The training of feeling and form should be balanced, but this balance is often upset when the adult mind is forced on the child. When feeling ceases then we have lost the flow to our bodies of the most important source of energy.

The influence of music on the movements of the body is only now being recognised. In music with strong rhythms, the discipline of time is stressed before the freedom of rhythm, constant practice being necessary to find this freedom. The help and co-operation of the musician would balance these sister arts.

Most dance teachers work under difficulties, as pupils may come from different environments and have not the same advantages. In my opinion we now need organised teachers who realise the value of forming groups. By making certain limitations, we could develop a uniformity of syllabus work for demonstration purposes. We would then discover the value of co-operation. It is the wrong approach to the syllabus that causes misunderstanding. The examinations will justify their existence if we use the syllabus as a dance language that must be mastered before one can make oneself articulate and express oneself freely within it.

When these basic foundations are part of dance training, there will be better material for the teacher of skilled techniques, which are necessary for the professional dancer. We are the stuff of which dance is made, and techniques do not exist if we do not master them. It is so true, that every artist is a technologist, every technologist is not an artist. The creative artist always leads.

The aims of the Stage Branch, as stated in the syllabus, can only materialise when we raise the standard of what I call the Common Sense of Dance. Do not hurry through examinations but take time to absorb, understand and experience the work that is stated on the syllabus. It is so distressing to see candidates doing work beyond their capabilities and lacking an intelligent understanding of their movements. There are endless possibilities within the Stage Branch just waiting to be developed.

Postscript

The ideals of Zelia are beautifully summed up in "The Common Sense of Dance" which is as valid in the fast pace of today as when she wrote it in 1949.

In all her lectures, teachings and writings she knew instinctively what one needed to become a dancer. She taught one to search for the true quality and meaning of dance; she taught one to be an individual.

Murielle Ashcroft.

Appendices

Key Dates in ISTD History

1902   First attempt to form society

1904   Imperial Society of Dance Teachers founded 25th July

      Ballroom Branch created, followed by Operatic Branch and General Branch

1924   Greek Dance Branch formed (October)

      Cecchetti Society Branch (November)

1925   Natural Movement Syllabus

1927   Natural Movement Branch (September)

1932   Stage Branch first committee announced in November

1933   Stage Branch first examinations in January

1945   ISTD incorporated

1947   Victorian and Sequence Branch (January)

      Latin American Branch (December)

1951   Greek Dance Association incorporated into ISTD

1952   Historical Dance Branch

      National Dance Branch

1953   Scottish Country Dance Branch (March)

1968   ISTD takes over administration of London College of Dance and Drama

1990   Dance Research Committee (Dance History Advisory Branch)

      Disco/Freestyle/Rock-n-Roll Branch

1998   South Asian Dance Faculty

1999   Alternative Rhythms Faculty

Imperial Society of Teachers of Dancing
Presidents and Chairmen

President		Chairman	
1904	RM Crompton		
1909-45	Major Cecil H Taylor		
		1945	Victor Silvester
1958	Victor Silvester	1958	CW Beaumont
		1970	Alex Moore
		1976	Diana Barker
1979	Alex Moore		
		1984	Beryl Grey
1991	Beryl Grey	1991	Joyce Percy
		2000	Robert Grover
2001	Bill Irvine		

Notes:

1. During the 1914-18 War, Mrs Bedford stood in for Major Taylor for a short time

2. in 1945 when the Society was incorporated the office of president was replaced by that of chairman.

3. in 1958 the office of President was created anew to honour the contribution of Victor Silvester

Imperial Society of Teachers of Dancing
Modern Theatre Faculty
(formerly Stage Branch)

Chairmen

1932	Zelia Raye
1957	Marjorie Davies and Olive Ripman (joint chairs)
1970	Shelagh Elliott-Clarke
1974	Murielle Ashcroft
1998	Patricia Crail